Why Have You Forsaken Me?

Why Have You Forsaken Me?

A Personal Reflection on the Experience of Desolation

John E. Colwell

Paternoster:
thinking faith

First published 2010 by Paternoster
Paternoster is an imprint of Authentic Media Limited
Milton Keynes
www.authenticmedia.co.uk

British Library Cataloguing in Publication Data

A catalogue record for this book is available from the
British Library

ISBN-13: 978-1-84227-684-6

Design by James Kessell for Scratch the Sky Ltd.
(www.scratchthesky.com)

Printed and bound in the UK by Bell & Bain Ltd., Glasgow

For Rosemary, Sarah, and Philip

Contents

Abbreviations

Throughout this book the following abbreviations are used:

ANF   *Ante-Nicene Father of the Christian Church*, 10 vols., eds. Alexander Roberts and James Donaldson (Edinburgh: T & T Clark/Grand Rapids, MI: Eerdmans, 1993–97 [1885–96]).

CD   Karl Barth, *Church Dogmatics*, vols. I–IV, Eng. trans. eds. G.W. Bromiley and T.F. Torrance (Edinburgh: T & T Clark, 1956–1975).

Institutes   John Calvin, *Institutes of the Christian Religion*, ed. J.T. McNeill, trans. F.L. Battles (Philadelphia: Westminster Press, 1960).

LW   Martin Luther, *Luther's Works* vols. 1–55, gen. ed. (vols. 1–30) Jaroslav Pelikan, gen. ed. (vols. 31–55) Helmut T. Lehmann (Philadelphia: Muhlenberg Press, 1955–75).

LXX   *Septuaginta* (one volume edition), ed. Alfred Rahlfs (Stuttgart: Deutsche Bibelgesellschaft, 1979).

𝔐   *Biblia Hebraica Stuttgartensia*, ed. Rudolf Kittel (Stuttgart: Deutche Bibelstiftung, 1967).

NPNF1 *The Nicene and Post-Nicene Fathers of the Christian Church*, First Series, 14 vols., ed. Philip Schaff *et al.*, (Edinburgh: T & T Clark/Grand Rapids, MI: Eerdmans, 1991–98 [1887–94]).

NPNF2   *The Nicene and Post-Nicene Fathers of the Christian Church*, Second Series, 14 vols., ed. Philip Schaff *et al.*, (Edinburgh: T&T Clark/Grand Rapids, MI: Eerdmans, 1994–98 [1887–94]).

ST   St. Thomas Aquinas, *Summa Theologica*, trans. by Fathers of the English Dominican Province (Westminster, Maryland: Christian Classics, 1981).

SJT   *Scottish Journal of Theology.*

Preface

This is not a book I want to write. Writing it has been on my mind for at least ten years. Several friends who know me well have urged me to write it. I think I may have something distinctive to say about the experience of depressive illness, about a psalm and its context, about the Cross of Christ, about the nature of God. But it is not a book I want to write and I have commandeered a host of excuses for postponing this beginning – there have always been other things to do, other projects to tackle. Even as now I make a beginning there is another project in my thoughts, on the unity of the virtues, that I really would prefer to tackle first. But friends and – more pertinently – my commissioning editor, are quite insistent.

All theology, of course, has a context: objective detachment is a foolish delusion that is neither desirable nor achievable; there is no theological reflection without a person reflecting, and that person has a story that has shaped them: a story that, in turn and inevitably, shapes their reflection, their speaking, and their writing. I have always tried to own my personal context and journey in the things that I have written: that I am a Christian Minister; that I am married, a father and a grandfather; that I am a Baptist; that I am English; that I have wrestled all my adult life with recurrent depression. These and so many other factors constitute who I am and thereby inform my approach to any theme. I cannot and would not want to deny any of these aspects of my life; I have disciplined myself to admit them, albeit in passing, in the course of most of that which I have written and certainly in my teaching within the College that I serve. Readers and hearers need to know that this is who I am and that my ideas and opinions are formed in this context and through this history.

But I hope I have never confused the context with the theme: theology (or, indeed, any other discipline) cannot be other than autobiographical, even if it is so unconsciously and unadmittedly, but theology must never degenerate into autobiography; the subject of theology is God, not the theologian, albeit that a theologian can only speak and write of God from a distinctive perspective. The temptation to draw attention to oneself, to one's own story, to one's own journey, to one's own prejudices – a temptation evident in all too many preachers – must be resisted.

Which is why I don't want to write this book, a book that necessarily is explicitly autobiographical in its beginning (though I hope that the explicitly autobiographical quickly will be superseded and displaced). I dread self-indulgence – but others must judge whether or not I succumb. I certainly am not attempting to portray myself as some 'wounded healer' – as I hope I make clear, there is only one wounded healer worthy of our attention; my only reason for telling something of my story is to introduce a focus on a telling of his story and its significance; I relate a context, not for its own sake, but for the sake of the one – the only one – who truly can transform any context.

The issue of dedication was a little problematic. In many respects I was drawn to dedicate the book to the two churches I have served as pastor that have loved me and therefore accepted me and coped with me both in my eccentricity and in my despair. As I mention later, there are those whom I have damaged and those to whom I am sorry. But equally I could dedicate the book to the College that employed me when it had so many excellent reasons not to do so and which has provided such a safe and affirming environment for life and thought and for precisely the theological reflection out of which this book and all my writing has been born. So many friends have been part of this journey that it is difficult (and probably wrong) to single any out – but Ian and Ros McFarlane have been more continually a part of the story than most and I treasure their friendship immensely. And as always, I am grateful to friends and colleagues who have encouraged this manuscript and commented on its development. In particular (and as already mentioned) I am grateful to Robin Parry, commissioning editor for Paternoster, for his insight and unfailing encouragement and to Kate Kirkpatrick for her diligent reading and for her helpful amendments to the text. As always, I am grateful to my colleague, Ian Randall, who has read the text as it developed and saved me from my worst blunders. I am grateful too, as in previous work, to Carolyn Evans, not just for her indexing and proofreading skills, but also for her acute theological insight. But, as always, my deepest gratitude – and therefore the dedication – belongs to my immediate family: to Rosie, my wife, who has loved me without faltering even in the darkest and most difficult places, and to my children, Sarah and Philip, who have borne with my strangeness and loved me even when I had given them cause to do otherwise – their mature friendship is more treasured than they can possibly realize.

Someone reading this book and wishing to avoid the autobiographical could, of course, skip the first two chapters, moving from the Introduction to Chapter Three and an engagement with the text of Psalm 22 and thereafter with questions of Christology and divine suffering. But such a strategy of avoidance might prove unsuccessful: the autobiographical cannot be so easily avoided; it is the inevitable context of all that here is discussed; theological reflection is necessarily personal and particular – and, for this reason (now that this book is finally being written), the autobiographical is unapologetic.

John E. Colwell
Easter 2009

Introduction

I really do not know how I would manage without Judy Powles, our College librarian: she is endowed with a patience that I do not possess and over and again she has pursued references and articles on my behalf that, left to my own devices, I would have simply omitted. I don't wish to try her patience (any more than I try her patience already) – but I really don't know how she (or any other librarian) will categorize this book. Moreover, this is not the first time that I have presented her with this sort of problem: *Living the Christian Story*[1] begins with a similar pondering of where it might fit in the standard Dewey Decimal System and *Rhythm of Doctrine*[2] could as easily be classified under liturgy as with other brief introductions to Christian doctrine. The problem with *Living the Christian Story* was that it fell into several categories. The problem with this present book is that it doesn't really fall into any category; it is far easier to determine what the book isn't than what it is.

As discussed in the preface, this book is not intended as a theological or spiritual autobiography; it is necessarily (and, I hope, appropriately) autobiographical but this is neither its focus nor its aim. The first two chapters offer some brief and very partial account of my own history with depressive illness – they are included not (I pray) to draw attention to myself through an extended and self-indulgent wallowing in pointless introspection and maudlin self-pity; they are included merely to identify my own particular context and circumstances as I come to read a psalm and to reflect upon it theologically. All theology is inevitably contextual – even when this remains unadmitted or when the intention has been to argue from objective detachment – theological reflection only occurs when there is a someone reflecting theologically and that someone comes with a particular and distinctive history and context. Objective detachment is not desirable because it is not achievable, it is not desirable because it is dishonest – albeit unwittingly dishonest through a lack of self-awareness. I do not come to this psalm as a reader in some form of hermetically-sealed vacuum, I come as the reader that I am, as the person that I am, with the perspective that is shaped by my context and history. I'm not trying to foist my context and history onto my readers – you can only come to read this book and the psalm on which it is a reflection as the person you are, with your distinctive history and context – I am merely trying to be honest about who I am, about my reasons for coming to read this psalm in the way that I read it and hear it, about my reasons for indwelling it and reflecting upon it in the way that I do. I am trying to be honest – but I could justly be accused of being less than honest; I leave a great deal of personal detail untold, partly in the perhaps futile attempt to avoid self-indulgence; partly simply for self-protection – I find it intensely painful to write this stuff (which is the reason I have put this off for so long); there is much in the more detailed and untold story that I regret and of which I am ashamed (since I have resolved never to use a form of illness as an excuse for otherwise inexcusable behaviour); and I have no wish to add to the hurt (my own and other people's) that has been an aspect and outcome of this history. I'm not disputing the legitimacy of autobiography (though I will never write one – for the reasons already stated and because I do not consider myself to be that interesting), but I doubt that any autobiography, less still biography, can ever be wholly revealing. For those more fascinated by autobiographical detail, there is already a more extensive, engaging, disturbing, and theologically reflective account of the experience of manic-depressive illness (bi-polar disorder) written by Kathryn Greene-McCreight[3] – though her experience, story, and symptoms are significantly different from my own (and I have lived with this now for more than thirty years and wonder whether she may have reflected on the experience prematurely). The first two chapters of this book, therefore, are inadequate and partial, an extended introduction rather than a focus, identifying the reader rather than the theme.

And following on from this qualifying of the autobiographical, this book is certainly not intended as some form of self-help manual, exploration of therapeutic techniques, or amateurish dabbling in pseudo-psychology. There are, no doubt, many books on the market that fall into such categories – it would be inappropriate for me to speculate on their value and I am thoroughly unqualified to attempt such a work. Again as I commented in the Preface to this book, I am not trying to present myself as some wounded healer – wounded maybe; healer certainly not. There is only one true wounded healer – only one, that is, who can truly heal us through his wounds – and he, rather than I, is the intended subject and focus of this extended reflection. I have had to learn the hard way that I am signally ill-equipped to heal anyone or even, in this particular, to participate very much as a means to that healing. No matter how deeply you experience depression, you never really come to understand it; you certainly cannot explain it to someone else. I understand what it feels like to be depressed, for this reason I can sympathize (if not empathize) with those suffering depression, but I cannot do much to help – in fact my attempt to help may well compound the problem. In spiritual naïveté I used to surmise that I might have been given to experience this in order to be able to help those who similarly suffered. I was wrong. If you do experience depressive illness and come to read this book please do not try to contact me thinking that I may be able to help. I can't. Talk with a pastor who knows you. Talk with a professional counsellor who has been recommended to you. Seek medical help (and don't feel any sense of spiritual failure in doing so). But don't contact me because I can't help you in the way that any of these others might be able to help you. Sometimes this wounded would-be healer is simply too wounded to be of any help. Too easily the quest for mutual understanding degenerates into a wallowing in mutual despair.

In essence and most basically, this book is an extended personal and theological reflection on Psalm 22. That it is (inevitably) a personal reflection is the justification and necessitation of the opening autobiographical chapters – I am trying to identify myself as the reader of this text, identifying my reasons for reading the text in the manner that I do, identifying the context from which I come to the text, identifying the questions and assumptions that I bring to the text. That it is (appropriately) a theological reflection is the justification for the final four chapters of the book (and readers should note, therefore, that the weight of the reflection falls here). That it is a reflection on this particular text is the justification for Chapters Three and Four; the justification for a detailed engagement with the text itself (noting what it is and also what it is not saying) and the justification for a pondering on the significance of the text in Israel's life and worship – and, thereby, a pondering on the significance of the text for the Church's life and worship. I can imagine, therefore, a well-meaning librarian categorizing the book within the commentary section of a theological library. But this book is not a commentary. I must tread carefully here: I am happily aware of the breadth, variety, imagination, and admitted responsiveness that has characterized some recent commentaries on the biblical text without any loss of concern to wrestle with the text in its detail – or to put the matter more briefly, I am aware of the impact of recent trends in hermeneutics on some recent biblical commentaries – but I am also aware that there remain some biblical scholars who reject such reflections as commentaries precisely because they are admittedly and self-consciously responsive and imaginative rather than an endeavour to analyse the text in detachment. Certainly the form of commentaries that dominated when I first began to study theology almost forty years ago (with one or two wonderful and refreshing exceptions) held detachment as an achievable virtue (rather than an unachievable vice), were concerned to excavate meaning rather than to explore significance, were preoccupied with that which lay behind the text – its possible author, original context and readers, its possible sources – almost at the expense of the text itself. This, obviously, is a far more complex debate than can be treated sufficiently here – though, in fact, this hermeneutical shift will be discerned by some to be underlying all that so far has been written – but I delight in this crumbling of the delusion of detachment. If a commentary is a detached analysis of the text then this is certainly not a commentary. If, however, a commentary is validly responsive, personal, and theologically reflective, an exploration of significance rather than a (probably futile) quest for original meaning, then maybe (by an extraordinary stretching of the category) this is a form of commentary.

I am aware too that, in the mind of some, I have no business to be writing any form of biblical commentary, even one so idiosyncratic; I am perceived to be a systematician, a theological ethicist, rather than a biblical scholar; I am beyond my comfort zone and beyond my expertise. Well firstly I must confess that whatever I am writing or teaching, and especially when I am preaching or trying to bring pastoral and spiritual direction to someone's life, I am continually and constantly beyond my comfort zone and beyond my expertise. I feel as foolish as Peter trying to walk on water, I expect to sink at any moment; I only make the attempt because Jesus beckons me. But I thoroughly reject the presumed compartmentalization that underlies the challenge and that still, regrettably, characterizes so many seminaries and theological departments. As a student of theology and of theological ethics (which is the worship, prayer, and discipleship of the Church), it is precisely my business and responsibility to engage with the biblical text, just as it is my responsibility to engage with the texts of the Christian tradition together with the texts that characterize the context in which that Christian tradition has developed. And, consequently, it should also be my responsibility to be competent in Greek, Hebrew, and Latin (not to mention German, French, and maybe a unmanageable host of other languages in which theological and philosophical thought has been expressed). No one person can be competent in everything – which is why I am constantly beyond my comfort zone and expect to sink at any moment – and for this reason members of a theological faculty need one another; the fulfilment of our own responsibilities is dependent upon the complementary skills of our colleagues; the culture of theological compartmentalization must be confronted and abolished for theology's sake, for the Church's sake, and for God's sake. Of course it is my business to write a commentary (though any form of commentary that I write will be similarly idiosyncratic) – but even with these considerations, I am still not convinced myself that this present book is really a commentary, even an idiosyncratic commentary.

The weight of the book, the final half of the book, is given to a theological reflection on the significance of the psalm, firstly in recognition that its opening words are repeated by Jesus on the Cross as witnessed by the Gospels of Matthew and Mark. The aim of Chapters Five and Six, consequently, is to reflect on the significance of these words of Jesus, and perhaps the entire psalm, for who he is, for his identification with us in our humanity, and for what happens on the Cross, for his identification with us in our sense of God-forsakenness. These words on Jesus' lips, especially when heard in the context of the psalm, have (I think) immense Christological and Soteriological significance, immense significance for how we understand the person of Jesus, his humanity and his deity, and immense significance for how we understand that which is accomplished through his incarnation, life, death, resurrection, and ascension. This book's reflection on Psalm 22 is explicitly and unapologetically Christological, yet this book falls far short of a Christology. I hope that, in my listening to the text of Psalm 22, I hear it in the context of every other text of Holy Scripture, of the Christian tradition (I certainly do not presume that I am the first Christian to wrestle with this text and to ponder its significance), and also of the manner in which the Church, in response to the text of Scripture including this psalm, has reflected on the significance of Christ's person and work. I hope this broader awareness is apparent in all I write (though in this book I am trying to keep footnotes to a minimum). But for this book to qualify as a Christology it would need a far broader focus, it would need to be a great deal longer, it would need to engage in detailed and sustained interaction with a wide range of thinkers throughout the Christian tradition, and it would need to address a series of questions that fall beyond its very limited scope. A proper Christology would be no less personal, for the reasons already expounded it could not be other than a personal response to a series of questions – albeit a personal response shaped by an indwelling of the Christian community and its sacramental life and worship, a personal response shaped in conscious conversation with the Christian tradition – but a proper Christology would require a far broader and more detailed series of conversations, giving similar focused attention to the totality of Scripture and the totality of the Christian tradition.

Inasmuch as the Church confesses Jesus Christ as truly God, inasmuch as God is defined through the gospel story, this book is a reflection on the nature of God as God is revealed in the Cross of Christ in the light of this psalm and its significance on the lips of the crucified Jesus. What does it mean for the one who is truly God to be God-forsaken? What does it mean for the one who is truly God to suffer and to die? What does it mean for the one who is truly God to be dead, to be buried in a tomb, anointed but left (apparently) to rot? What might all this signify for our understanding of who God is, for our understanding of what this word 'God' might mean? This book, though a very personal reflection on a psalm, cannot avoid these immense questions, but – through its confessed limitations and distinctive focus – it can barely begin to address such questions. Largely and increasingly through the second half of the twentieth century – though, in fact, with roots much earlier – much has been written on the supposed suffering of God and of the implications this might have for God's relatedness to time (an understanding of eternity) and his changelessness. I hope that, in Chapter Seven of this book, I demonstrate an awareness of these trends and of my considered response to them (again a personal response shaped by a series of conversations within the Christian tradition and with close theological friends), but within the scope of a single chapter I cannot hope to do justice to such a far-reaching and complex question; this certainly is not a book about the supposed suffering of God; such full and detailed discussion must also be postponed to a later and very different work.

And this book is not a sustained discussion of divine suffering because, as Chapter Eight clarifies, from my very personal perspective this is not the primary or most pressing question raised by the psalm as it is interpreted in the light of the Cross. In this respect, Chapter Eight returns us to the end of Chapter Two (albeit in the light of a series of Christological, soteriological, and theological reflections) and to the more pressing personal question of finding God in the darkness, of finding God in the very experience of apparent God-forsakenness. For this reason this book could be categorized as an exploration of spirituality, an exploration of the 'dark night of the soul' – and maybe, therefore, this is where the book properly belongs within a library – but even this designation is not unproblematic or incontestable. That which St John of the Cross (1542–1591) means by depression is certainly not what I mean by depression throughout this book.[4] St John of the Cross speaks of melancholia or depression as the disillusionment that may come early in a Christian's walk when the true cost of discipleship begins to dawn – quite rightly St John of the Cross distinguishes this immature disillusionment from the dark night of seeming God-forsakenness that, in actuality, is a mark and stage of spiritual maturity. I think I want to conclude that clinical depression can constitute what St John of the Cross (and the Christian tradition more generally) intends by the dark night of the soul but I must qualify this by the recognition that not all clinical depression has this spiritual significance or admits to this spiritual interpretation and, correspondingly, certainly not every experience that can be termed the dark night of the soul has its roots in clinical depression. Whether for me the experience of clinical depression constitutes what St John of the Cross meant by the dark night of the soul is impossible for me to answer – I suspect that there have been times when this has been the case and times when it hasn't. But this book is about a personal spiritual walk in the light of this psalm and its significance and, for this reason, if it belongs anywhere, it belongs in the spirituality section of a theological library.

My concern, then, in writing this book and in reading this psalm (other than the simple fact that it is Holy Scripture) is to reflect on the felt experience of God-forsakenness, my own and that of Christ in the light of this psalm; to explore the theological and spiritual significance of this felt experience for myself, for Christ, for Christians generally. If this exploration proves to be helpful to me or to others then obviously I am glad (I certainly am not intending to be unhelpful to myself or to others – though I recognize the risk of such), but I am not writing this book to be helpful but rather to be truthful (and perhaps hopeful). This is a personal journey of reflection with a psalm which I invite you, the reader, to share if you will.

Chapter One

Into The Darkness

Your wrath has swept over me;
    your terrors have destroyed me.
All day long they surround me like a flood;
    they have completely engulfed me.
You have taken my companions and loved ones from me;
    the darkness is my closest friend. (Psalm 88:16–18)

I can't remember much of the conversation in that consulting room – indeed, I can't remember with clarity much at all that happened in those months in 1974 – just a few words lodged in my mind: manic depression; cyclic illness; probably regular periods of hospitalization; lithium carbonate. I was sitting in a consulting room in Colchester Hospital, confused, tearful, desolate. My GP had arranged an appointment with a consultant psychiatrist and this was his diagnosis – about as devastating as the symptoms that had brought me there.

Looking back on my childhood, and especially on my teenage years, I guess the diagnosis explains much which, though mild in comparison, was odd and sometimes disturbing. I was an only child in a loving (and certainly over-protective) devoutly Christian home. I was always a loner; always more content with my own company than in the company of others (with only a few exceptions); always given to tantrums; always just a little obsessive; always liable to become agitated, over-excited, and over-enthusiastic. Grammar school had been a largely unhappy and unfruitful experience. Until I began to respond to a sense of call to Christian ministry my life had been directionless and mostly 'grey', but it was not until I was a theological student that depression began to take a hold. In the summer vacation of 1972 I had a driving job, delivering photographic equipment to retailers in Kent and Sussex. I would be driving from one delivery point to another weeping uncontrollably for no apparent reason. I was scared. I didn't know why I was crying. I wasn't consciously unhappy about anything (I had just got engaged to the woman who would become my wife). I wasn't consciously worried about anything (to my great surprise – having squandered an excellent education – I seemed to be progressing well at college). I was just weeping uncontrollably without knowing why. In my frightened confusion I went to see the one who then was my GP – which proved to be a big mistake. I had known this doctor all my life. He had brought me into the world. I counted him a friend. And he could not have been less sympathetic, bemoaning how depressive the world seemed to have become (I discovered later that his own son had only just been confined in hospital with serious mental illness and he himself gave up general practice a few months later having had some form of 'breakdown'). He gave me a prescription for Valium which I tore up as I went out of the door. As the summer passed so did the tears and I settled back to my studies.

In June of the following year Rosemary and I married but as the summer progressed the sense of despair returned, though not as acutely as before and without the uncontrollable weeping. I broached the subject with a local Baptist Minister who had some part-time responsibility at the college where I was studying and who was about as unhelpful as my GP – he dabbled in Jungian psychology and seemed to see me as a guinea pig (I may be being unfair, but that is how it felt at the time). As autumn progressed the sense of despair again lifted and I immersed myself in Hebrew and Greek texts as I prepared for finals. That first year of marriage some would count as strange: Rosie would go to work; I would study all day; I (usually) would cook a (very simple) meal in the evening, I would then sit down with the Hebrew or Greek text while Rosie would check my reading with my own previous English translation. Study was unremitting.

Joey, the man who had been best man at our wedding, had been my closest friend during my late teenage years. He was not an only child but he was an 'after-thought', having a significantly older brother and sister. Coincidentally his mother and my mother had been close friends when they were teenagers. For several years we had been virtually inseparable. Early that next summer he broke his neck in a gym accident and, ever since, he has been paralysed from his neck downwards. I felt completely numb. At about the same time a former Sunday-School teacher, another friend of the family, hanged herself for no apparent reason. I didn't see her hanging (it was her brother who found her) but for weeks I couldn't erase the imagined image from my mind.

That summer we moved to my first pastorate. That summer Rosie discovered she was pregnant with our first child. That summer the depression – though perhaps now I should say the madness – overwhelmed me as never before. I became pathologically obsessive about the most trivial details of life. I would fly into frightful and frightening rages for little reason. I would swing from eccentric enthusiasm and overflowing self-confidence to extremes of inexplicable despair and self-loathing. And the weeping returned. At first Rosie would make excuses for me, trying to protect me from visitors and from the inevitable claims on my time, but quickly it became impossible to hide the fact that something was seriously wrong. The GP I saw now was wonderfully sympathetic and reassuring: she immediately made an appointment for me to see a psychiatrist; she gave me a prescription for anti-depressants and sedatives – and this time I took the tablets – but a week later she had to double the dose.

And through all this Rosie coped – she coped with a new home, a new church, with pregnancy, and with me (though it's not easy to cope with a husband who has become convinced that you are poisoning him). To my shame, I didn't realize at the time quite what a remarkable person I had married. Rosie coped, but she was very tired, extraordinarily tired, and so she too visited the doctor and was discovered to have a growth in her thyroid gland that severely limited its function. Incidentally, this remains one of the few instances of 'miraculous' healing that I have witnessed – the consultant surgeon was hesitant to operate because of the proximity of the growth (which might have proved benign) to Rosie's vocal chords, yet four years later there was no growth and Rosie's thyroid gland was functioning normally (and has done so ever since).

And so, once every month, Rosie and I travelled to Colchester, she to the oncology department to ensure that the lump wasn't growing, I to the psychiatric department to ensure that my moods were stabilizing. I am one of the fortunate people for whom Lithium works (works, not in the sense of a 'cure' but in the sense of an effective means of limiting the extremes of mood swing) but Lithium takes a while to build up in the blood stream, so initially I was on an even greater dose of anti-depressants. While I usually saw a registrar or other assistant, I am enormously grateful for the kindness and patience of the psychiatrist to whom I was assigned. There was one occasion when, convulsing in tears, I telephoned his secretary who put me through to him and he spoke to me over the phone, seemingly unhurriedly, trying to calm me down. Why he didn't have me sectioned there and then I will never know (but I'm glad he didn't). I suspect the only reason that I stayed out of hospital was that a deacon of the church and his wife invited us to stay with them for a couple of months (until the Lithium began to take effect) – I misused their kindness in so many ways but to them, above anyone else besides Rosie, I am incalculably grateful.

That year, the summer of '74 to the summer of '75, was an extraordinary catalogue of events: finals, a disabled best friend, a suicide, a new church, a new home, pregnancy, the diagnosis of manic depression, thyroid problems, and (just in case our cup was not already overflowing) Rosie's parents, after years of cheerless marriage, decided to divorce. Obviously I contemplated resigning from the pastorate (though as to where and how we would have lived I had no idea) but several factors dissuaded us. In the first place (and as already mentioned), Lithium 'kicked in' and my mood stabilized; life, at least to some minimal degree, became manageable. Secondly, and perhaps most remarkably, this horrendous year was punctuated with a couple of moments of spiritual renewal (to which I will return in the next chapter), leaving us both with the sense that possibly there may yet be something that we could bring to the body of Christ. But most decisively, this church that had only just called me to be pastor, that barely knew us, nonetheless seemed to love us unconditionally and bore patiently with my total absence for four months when we had barely arrived, and then with my continued strangeness and unpredictability. I'm sure there are churches that wouldn't have responded so graciously and magnanimously – and I couldn't have blamed them – but this little church was exemplary in its love and care. Maldon remains one of my favourite places on earth, with surprisingly happy memories. It was about this time that I first met Colin Gunton (then a junior lecturer in philosophy of religion at King's College, London) and discovered that further academic study – and writing in particular – was therapeutic rather than problematic, renewing rather than stress inducing.

Unless you have experienced some form of clinical depression you probably have no inkling of the breadth of the symptoms. It isn't just a matter of unimaginable despair and inexplicable weeping or blank numbness. There is, of course, the recurring temptation to suicide (quite a few people view suicide as the ultimate selfish act but, in this instance, they could not be more wrong: the depressive isn't drawn to suicide simply because they feel they can't face life anymore; the depressive is drawn to suicide because they genuinely believe that the world would be a better place if they were no longer in it; the depressive believes they would be doing a favour to those they love by exiting life). But beyond the obvious there are physical symptoms: intense weariness; a digestive system on overdrive; a distinctive headache in the form of a feeling of weight pressing on your head; a dryness in the mouth and unquenchable thirst; and a complete inability to concentrate (at my very worst, I couldn't read a page of Enid Blyton and tell you what I had read). And, for me, there is acute people-phobia: again at my worst Rosie had almost to frog-march me up the High Street in order to confront the sheer terror of meeting people; I could lead worship and preach long before I felt at ease saying good-bye to people at the door; even at my best I dread having to socialize with people I don't really know (I keep my friends close); and a church social is my idea of Purgatory. I suspect that others who suffer depression could list rival collections of physical symptoms. But at least you know (or come to know) when you are depressed. Initially, at least, you have no idea when you are manic: suddenly you feel on great form; you can't understand why everyone else doesn't share your enthusiasm and seemingly boundless energy; you cannot understand why others do not feel as intensely (in reality, as obsessively) as you feel; you are passionate about everything and everyone, loving and loathing in equal exaggerated measure; you think you're being interesting, in fact you're being outrageous. All these symptoms, for me, were brought under control by Lithium. Apart from one more minor 'episode' in the summer of 1976 I remained stable. So imagine the horror of my GP when, after barely two years of continuous stability and no longer seeing the psychiatrist on a regular basis, I announced that I wanted to stop taking the tablets.

Lithium worked for me, but Lithium is problematic. Simply physically, Lithium can do damage to liver and kidneys, and every month I had a blood test to check the level of Lithium in my system. But more pressingly, I was stable but I felt truncated. A while ago, Stephen Fry presented a series of two programmes on British television on the subject of manic depression (bipolar disorder):[1] he spoke of his own experience and he interviewed several others who had experienced some form of the illness; one of these interviewees described being on Lithium as being 'letter-boxed' – when some films, shot in wide-screen format, are shown on television, the top and the bottom of the television screen are blanked-out – that is precisely what it feels like to be on Lithium, the extremes of mania and despair have gone, but so has about a third of your personality; you feel temperamentally castrated. Consequently, for those (like me) who suffer only a mild form of the illness, there is a choice to be made between the effects of the treatment and the torment of the illness itself. Surprisingly (perhaps), only one of all those interviewed by Stephen Fry wanted to be other than they were: you cannot remove the problem without also removing those distinctive characteristics that make you the person you are (this also I will revisit in the next chapter).

At the time of writing, I have not taken Lithium for almost thirty years; there have certainly been times when I have needed some form of drug therapy to calm me down, but I have avoided Lithium (and, thus far, I have avoided hospitalization). A later GP (who was also a friend and colleague in the second church I served as pastor) queried the original diagnosis – people do not recover from manic depression. He may, of course, be right; the psychiatrist I then saw, and my GP at the time, may have been wrong. Certainly I know people diagnosed as manic depressive who are considerably more obviously ill than I have ever been, who have been regularly sectioned, and who have spent long spells in hospital, whose manic phases (at least) are more extreme than anything I have known – the label bi-polarity seems to be given to those suffering similar symptoms but with differing intensity. My purpose in writing this account is not to defend a diagnosis (in most respects I have a vested interest in discarding the diagnosis – in some respects it's helpful to have a label, but in most respects it's a handicap, especially if you regularly admit it); my purpose in writing this account is simply to describe a set of symptoms (whatever medical label may be appropriate) in order to explain why I come to a particular psalm, to the Cross of Christ, and to the entirety of Christian faith and discipleship, in the manner that I do. All this is inextricably part of the person (and the reader of Scripture) that I am.

But more pointedly, as my closest family and friends will tell you, I have certainly not 'recovered', I've just spent thirty years developing strategies for coping. And if it weren't for the insight, patience, wisdom, resilience, and dogged determination of Rosie in particular, then my lack of 'recovery' would be all too obvious, I probably would have been hospitalized, or (and more probably) the temptation to sit in the garage with the car's engine running, or to swallow rather too many tablets, would have proved irresistible.

Leaving Maldon was one of the hardest things I have ever done. Like all churches, it was not without its frustrations and awkward personalities (it was a church that did not easily warm to the notion of change) – but I have never felt more loved and accepted by any community of God's people. Nonetheless, there were regrettable associations and, more positively, I was being encouraged by my former College Principal and by others to take time out from pastoral ministry and to give time to further study. So, after not a little prevarication, we moved back to south London and to a flat made available by Spurgeon's College – a flat that somehow accommodated me, Rosie, our two small children, a golden retriever, a cat, a piano, and all the other furniture we had accumulated in a medium-sized Manse. Several friends from the church in Maldon and elsewhere supported us (in more than the obvious ways), the College provided us with accommodation and 'pocket money' in exchange for some Old Testament teaching, and I pursued research as an external student of King's College, London with Colin Gunton as my supervisor. We had sufficient (though very little) and we were idyllically happy – but my extreme mood swings continued (though not as severely as over the previous few years).

It was during this period that I became increasingly overtly involved in the charismatic movement – though this involvement actually dates back to a spiritual experience when I was seventeen that, in some respects, had been renewed during that dreadful first year in Maldon. Just a moment's reflection will alert any perceptive reader to a not insignificant difficulty: if, as an aspect of an illness, you are given to 'manic' phases such as those I have described previously, how do you distinguish such clinical mania from authentic ecstatic spiritual experience? I don't have a simple answer to the question: I recognize that the Holy Spirit does extraordinary, surprising, and sometimes strange things in people's lives (if you doubt this, re-read Ezekiel sometime); I'm certainly not dismissive of felt experience; but I have learnt (again the hard way) to be distrustful of my own felt experience. Sadly, I did learn this the hard way and, as a consequence, I'm sure there are people I damaged (especially in the second church where I was pastor) because I hadn't sufficiently refined this suspicion, because I confused mania with inspiration.

When we moved to Catford (still in south London) for me to serve as pastor in what was then known as Catford Hill Baptist Church, I had about three months' work still to complete for my doctoral dissertation. A year later I still had three months' work to complete, and, were it not again for the kindness of friends who allowed me to be a recluse in their home for a month (to finish three months' work in that month) the dissertation would never have been finished (and my subsequent story may have been very different). And once again in that month I learnt (for me) the therapeutic benefits of focused study. Catford is a very different place to Maldon and the church in Catford similarly could not have been more different. Reflecting some years later on the two churches that I have served as pastor it is the second, in outward terms at least, that has been the more fruitful and effective. Long after my leaving (and partly perhaps as an outcome of my leaving) it continues to flourish. But this was at extraordinary cost. From the very beginning life was filled with tension, overt opposition, and conflict. I am sure that some of that conflict and tension was of my own making. I had not yet learnt sufficiently to recognize the signs of manic obsessions and enthusiasms (maybe I am still learning to recognize those signs) but many of the tensions were inherent in the church as it was and as it developed. It is neither helpful nor presently pertinent to relate the story in any detail (and I still don't have confidence in my own assessment – or even awareness – of all that occurred). Suffice it to say that, in the twelve years that we were there, I was regularly out of action for a month or so, and (if we include a three month sabbatical) I was only present and fit for work for about six months of the final two years of the pastorate. Much of this can be attributed simply to stress – and maybe anyone in this situation would have needed time out – but the situation was massively compounded by my continuing condition. Neither there nor anywhere else (since those very early days in Maldon) have I been secretive about recurrent depression and the original diagnosis – but maybe it is easier for folk to conclude that their pastor is suffering from stress than that he really is rather more seriously and chronically ill.

Eventually, and with the advice and encouragement of my GP, I came to recognize that I would not recover from that current crisis unless I resigned from the pastorate. I resigned with immense reluctance: notwithstanding the continuing tensions, I loved the people; I was honoured to work with my colleagues; I felt I was failing them – but I realized that I would be failing them more by staying than by going. And in my going the church could not have been more generous: I resigned in the October but they continued to pay a full salary until the following May when I began work at Spurgeon's College (and I suspect they would have continued to pay me for longer), and we continued to live in the Manse until, over a year after resigning, we were able to move to a new home. I'm sure there are ministers who are treated abominably by churches, just as I am sure that there are churches that are treated abominably by ministers, but the former, at least, has never been my experience. We have so many continuing and precious friendships from both these churches and, indeed, from so many other churches that in less prominent ways have been part of our story. I have little patience with ministers who moan about churches: Jesus loved the Church and gave himself up on the Cross for the Church (Ephesians 5:25); the Church is precious to him and the Church should always be precious to us.*

---

* By the time this book came to publication the author, while remaining Senior Research Fellow at Spurgeons College, had returned to local church pastoral ministry as Minister of Budleigh Salterton Baptist Church, Devon.

As I intimated in the Preface, I can think of lots of reasons why Spurgeon's College should never have employed me: though my doctorate had been published and though I had published several articles since then, I was still relatively unproven as an academic; I had recently had to resign from a pastorate through ill-health; the nature of that ill-health was known to the College; I was still taking medication when I came for interview (and for the first few months of employment). And while I was relieved to have a job and to be no longer dependent on the extraordinary generosity of the church at Catford, for the early months of my time at Spurgeon's that is how I viewed it, as a 'job'. I never really wanted to leave Catford; I clung to the possibility (no matter how remote and foolish) that it may have proved possible to return; I didn't really want to be an academic (it may seem bizarre to some, but I study because I enjoy studying and because, as I've already noted, I find it therapeutic); I believed (and still believe) that God had called me and separated me to be a Christian pastor. It took a year, perhaps longer, to come to understand that I was still fulfilling that calling, albeit in a different context and a different manner. I enjoy reading, teaching, and writing so much that sometimes I have to pinch myself to remind myself that I am being paid to do this. As with any responsibility there are less happy aspects – marking becomes wearisome through its sheer quantity and, as in any lively community, there are political and personal frustrations – but the College remains an immensely happy place.

But the recurrent depression and the recurrent mania continue, though surprisingly unnoticed because surprisingly unobtrusive. One of the key differences between ministry in the College and ministry in the pastorate is that in the former you can effectively go home. When I first returned to the College, Rosie and I would come home after work, enjoy a meal, wash up, and then sit down and wonder what normal people did with an evening – evenings didn't happen in the pastorate. Ministry at the College has clearly marked boundaries (and generous vacations and sabbaticals that can be devoted to reading and writing with little interruption). Even at my lowest I can pace myself (with not a little help from Rosie and from colleagues), I can psych myself up sufficiently to cope with a lecture or seminar and postpone almost everything else until the darkness lifts. Most of the time most students and even most of my colleagues just think I'm overtired, unsociable, and short-fused – though I'm honest about depression people generally don't recognize the symptoms for what they are. For three years I was Academic Dean: I'm a competent administrator (though not remotely as competent as the present incumbent), I treat the planning of timetables as I treat cryptic crosswords (as a puzzle to be solved) and maybe being a little obsessive helps – but the final months in the post and the six months following were the bleakest time I have known since being at the College. And if being a little obsessive helped then, being a little manic helps most of the time. I'm paid to be outrageous. I'm paid to excite, to infuriate, and to disturb. I'm paid to make students think. The outrageousness that would be an offensive vice in a local church is an engaging virtue in a college. And even now I don't always know myself whether the outrageousness is 'controlled' or manic. Sometimes it feels as if I am outside of myself, one step removed from myself, listening to myself saying outrageous things. Sometimes I will apologize to a class in case I was 'over the top'. Sometimes I will ask a student I know well whether I was more than a little eccentric. Sometimes a colleague will gently mention that I'm being a little loud and intrusive. And I've learnt to be grateful for such warnings and to heed them. As I said previously, I have lived with depression long enough to know when I am depressed but I still need help to recognize when I'm manic – though maybe I should be grateful that I have remained (or become) sufficiently sane to be grateful for the hints, especially from Rosie, that I might be speaking and acting a little strangely. And as I also have said previously, I have learnt not fully to trust my own feelings and enthusiasms.

Reflecting on the last thirty years, in some respects the depression has eased somewhat – I am rarely rendered completely numb and incapable; I rarely now descend to uncontrollable weeping (though it still can happen) – but in other respects it is worse in the sense that it is more continuous – there used to be periods when I felt entirely 'normal' but now, even at the best of times, the darkness is a lingering presence on the margins of my mind, never wholly absent, always threatening. And in some ways more troubling, I live with the fear that, as I grow older, my ability to keep the bizarre stuff that goes on in my head from infringing on reality will give way – if this should occur then medication or confinement would become a necessity.

So far in this account I've not mentioned my children. They are adults now but their childhood was blighted by the presence of a disturbingly unpredictable father. Maybe it was an inherent generosity of spirit, maybe it was the potency of their mother's ability to cope, but Sarah and Philip are now (and have always been) unfailingly sympathetic, forgiving, and supportive. As adults they are our closest friends and confidants. They each have pastoral gifts that significantly exceed my own. Maybe children are always more resilient than we expect.

This chapter began with the closing verses of a psalm the final line of which psalm provides the title for Kathryn Greene-McCreight's account of her experience of manic depression, *Darkness is my only companion.*[2] Of all the psalms of lament it is probably the bleakest. It seems entirely devoid of hope. All that is left is despair and desolation. But maybe even this psalm, for all its despair, is not entirely hopeless. It is, after all, a prayer. It is addressed to God even though it betrays no assurance that God is listening. Maybe all the while the psalmist expresses complaint in a prayer, all the while the despair is directed to God, for all the lack of assurance and comfort, there is still an ember of hope.[3] And what a strange and enigmatic way for the psalm to end. The Hebrew can be translated otherwise ('my friends are darkness' or 'my friends are in darkness');[4] but if we stay with this more common translation, can it really be that the darkness itself can become a friend?

Dear Lord,
sometimes you lead us in green pastures and beside still waters,
sometimes you restore our souls;
but sometimes you hold us in the presence of enemies,
and sometimes we find ourselves in valleys of darkness.
You say you will be with us, to guide and to comfort,
but we don't always feel your presence,
and we never see your form.
Teach us to trust you when we cannot see and cannot feel;
hold us when we cannot hold onto you.
For the sake of the one who entered our darkness,
and who cried in desolation;
even your beloved Son.
Amen.

Chapter Two

Reflecting on the Darkness

... there was given me a thorn in my flesh, a messenger of Satan, to torment me. Three times I pleaded with the Lord to take it from me. But he said to me, 'My grace is sufficient for you, for my power is made perfect in weakness.' Therefore I will boast all the more gladly about my weaknesses ...

(2 Corinthians 12:7–9)

I must have pleaded far more than three times for this darkness to be taken away but, as yet, it has not been. We could argue fruitlessly for ages concerning the nature of Paul's 'thorn in the flesh', whether or not it was some form of sickness – but the point is, surely, that whatever it was God did not take it away; God left Paul in this continuing weakness. And maybe in the previous chapter I have been guilty of 'boasting' about my weakness – though 'boasting' hardly seems the appropriate word.

If you grew up in the spiritual context in which I grew up you certainly would not be 'boasting' of your weaknesses, at least, not this particular weakness. I vaguely remember that, in the Mission Hall that my parents then attended (in the 1950s), there was a young woman who suffered some form of 'nervous breakdown' (as we used to term it) and had to spend a short time in psychiatric hospital (or the 'asylum' as even then it was still popularly known). I can still remember, even though I was a child, the hushed and embarrassed tones in which people talked about her – the only near-equivalent reaction within that church was when another young woman had the temerity to sue for divorce. Back in the England of the '50s certain things didn't happen to good evangelical Christians, and 'nervous breakdowns' was one of them. Even in the early 1970s, when I came home weeping from that driving job, and later when my illness was diagnosed, my parents (who were truly loving and devoted parents) didn't know how to handle it: they assumed I'd just been overdoing things; they assumed it would quickly pass; they had no notion of the mental mess that was me. The remarkable thing, as I noted in the previous chapter, is that in neither of the Baptist churches where I have served as pastor – or, indeed, in any other of the churches which have played some part in our later journey – have I encountered any form of prejudice or censure.

The initial problem, of course, was my own prejudice. I may have been a 'loner' as a child. I may always have had a 'short fuse'. I may have been a little obsessive and slightly strange in other ways. But I hadn't been depressed (or, at least, I hadn't been aware of being depressed). I hadn't been mad. This sort of thing didn't happen to good evangelical Christians (not that I ever have been a 'good' evangelical Christian), and it certainly didn't happen to charismatic Christians. Something must be spiritually wrong. There must be some wilful disobedience or unconfessed sin somewhere (as if there were ever a time when there was not some lingering sin or disobedience). For all these reasons my initial reaction to what was happening to me in 1974 was to tell as few people as possible, to relate to them as little as possible, and to dissemble as much as possible (or to lie, in other words). Until it became impossible to hide what was happening to me, I (or Rosie) would tell folk that I was overtired, or had some form of tummy-bug, or had a cold. I couldn't cope with admitting to myself, less still other people, that I was mentally sick. So of course I asked God to take it away, time and time again.

Barely a moment's reflection should be sufficient for anyone to recognize the foolishness of such prejudice. We do not feel any sort of spiritual failure if we break a leg (unless we were doing something we shouldn't have been doing at the time). We don't feel we have failed God if we have a heart attack, or ulcers, or cancer – though any one of these sicknesses can be at least partly self-induced. The brain is the most complex organ of the body; we still have relatively very little understanding of quite how it functions (or, more philosophically, of what actually we mean by the word 'mind'); it would be extraordinary if this most complex organ, like the heart, liver, or kidneys, did not sometimes malfunction in some way. As a friend of mine would put it: we should be grateful that the whole of life isn't unending toothache. Realizing (and admitting) that I was simply ill eventually came to be the most basic means by which I came to cope with the condition: I'm just ill; there's nothing spiritually wrong (or, at least this is not what this is about); there's no hidden sin (well, probably there is, but again this is not what this is about); I'm just ill; there is a chemical imbalance in my brain and Lithium counteracts it (why else would Lithium 'work'?).

But, of course, without necessarily a prejudice against mental illness, there have been plenty of people who have assumed that I should be healed. You cannot participate in the charismatic movement without being encountered by people who believe that you should be healed, who believe that everyone should be healed, who assume that Paul's 'thorn in the flesh' could not possibly have been a sickness of any kind.

By far the most problematic of these well-intentioned (but deeply misguided) people are those who assume that mental illness (or, at least, this mental illness) is demonic. Indeed, I would be surprised if there were not some who, reading the previous chapter, did not arrive at this conclusion: here is someone who can speak of a presence of darkness, who feels invaded and overwhelmed, who can almost observe himself doing and saying outrageous things – clearly a case of demonization. Such people, I am sure, are entirely unaware of the unimaginable damage that they can inflict – or at least, this is what I assume: if they are aware of the damage they can cause, if they even have an inkling of that damage and yet persist in their assumption, then it is they rather than I who ought to be locked up.

I must admit that more than once, in depressive desperation, I have submitted myself to so-called deliverance ministry. And I must similarly admit that, of course, I was not 'delivered' – though mercifully the problem wasn't compounded (it was already dreadful – if this had not been the case I wouldn't have ventured down this pathway in the first place). But, of course, some who hold this view would say that I wasn't delivered because I lacked the faith, or because I was holding on to my demon for some reason. So it's my fault (as if I already didn't have enough problems). Ho hum!

I realize that it is bound to alienate some readers but, in very recent years, I have grown increasingly agnostic about demons. Previously I would not have questioned their reality: demons and deliverance are included in the testimony of Scripture and that is the end of the matter. Or is it? Principally there are two bases on which Christians continue to argue for the reality of demons. On the one hand (though very much secondarily) it is argued that some contemporary phenomena cannot be explained in any other way. This is an entirely unconvincing argument. All such phenomena can be and are explained in other ways. The symptoms can be explained by modern psychiatry (I'm not assuming that simply because modern psychiatry is 'modern' it is necessarily correct – I'm merely saying that it offers coherent alternative explanation). The phenomena of 'deliverance', in most cases, can be attributed to the power of suggestion (particularly with respect to mentally and emotionally vulnerable people). And where such deliverance issues in genuine and lasting healing (which I suspect is rare, if the truth be told), can we not simply accept that the gracious God brought healing regardless of our false assumptions? If God waited to act until we arrived at an entirely proper understanding no miracle of healing would ever occur.

However, for Christians, overwhelmingly the primary ground for accepting the reality of demons and of deliverance is that they occur in Scripture and, in particular, in the ministry of Jesus. But are we thereby claiming that the understanding of the biblical writers and of biblical characters (including Jesus) must be absolutely accurate by virtue of the fact that this is recorded in Scripture? Are we claiming that the effect of the Holy Spirit's inspiration (in whatever form it took) was to extract writers and characters from their immediate context and cultural understanding? Are we really claiming that because Jesus speaks of a grain of wheat falling into the ground and dying (John 12:24) that modern biological accounts of germination are incorrect? Jesus is not recorded as commenting on the matter, but there is little reason to suppose that he wouldn't have assumed the sun to circle the earth. Jesus wouldn't have been able to give a lecture on quantum mechanics – and to assume that he would have been able to do so constitutes a denial of his true humanity and a misunderstanding of the implications of his true deity. The eternal Son doesn't just assume human flesh, he assumes particular human flesh, Jewish human flesh, male human flesh, first-century human flesh, with all the limitations and particularities of context and culture this implied. His identity as the eternal Son was continuous but without prejudice to the limitations of the real humanity he assumed. If he knew something that others did not know, he did so because the Father (by the Spirit) made it known to him (John 14:10). He was and is truly God, but as one who is and was truly human he grew as we grow, he learnt things as we learn them, he was (and remained) ignorant of other things just as we remain ignorant of some things.[1] And accordingly it is entirely reasonable (and not at all faithless) to suppose that he would have assumed an understanding of the 'spiritual world' and an understanding of specific illnesses that was common to his cultural context.

As John Calvin recognizes,[2] God accommodates himself to the people to whom he is revealing himself – were this not the case, revelation would not be at all revealing. When the Bible speaks of the sun stopping in the sky (Joshua 10:12f.), the moon giving its light (Isaiah 60:19), the roots of the mountains (Job 28:9), the waters above the heavens (Genesis 1:6), when the Bible speaks (as we still speak) of a man sowing his seed in a woman (and assumes that childlessness is always attributable to a woman's 'barrenness' rather than a man's impotence), all this (while perhaps metaphorical) reflects the particular cultural contexts in which God made himself known to actual men and women. The Bible witnesses to God's truth but it does so within the limitations of human language to a particular people with their particular understandings and suppositions. We must not confuse the language with the truth (which ultimately is irreducibly personal) – though the truth as it is given to us is inseparable from the language of Scripture. We must not confuse the humanity of Christ with his deity (we will return to this question in Chapters Five and Seven) – though neither may we separate Christ's deity from the humanity in which it is revealed. When Jesus permits the demons to enter a herd of pigs and they hurtle over a cliff and into the sea (Mark 5:11ff.), God *may* be accommodating a miraculous healing to the understanding and assumptions of this particular crowd at this particular time (and similarly even to the particular understanding and assumptions of the Son in his assumed and real humanity). I'm not saying that this was the case (as I said earlier, I have become agnostic in this respect); I am merely saying that I can think of no good theological reason why it should not be the case.

Demons are seemingly everywhere in the Gospels (or, at least, in the synoptic Gospels) and, to some degree, in Acts. They don't really figure in the Old Testament,[3] nor do they really figure in the letters of the New Testament. The standard explanation for this apparent absence and presence is that it was the presence of Christ (and the earliest phase of the Church's life) that brought these hostile powers into the open. This is entirely plausible – but no more plausible (and probably less plausible) than the possibility that the prominence of demons within the Gospels simply reflects the dominant distinctive culture of Second Temple Judaism, a culture significantly shaped by assumptions concerning a spiritual world that flourished earlier in the Persian Empire.[4] Perhaps, consequently, it is not insignificant that contemporary Christian awareness of the demonic tends to surface in cultures already characterized by such assumptions concerning a spirit world. Christian tradition has identified demons as fallen angels but this tradition, ancient and strong as it may be, is entirely without clear biblical foundation and is not theologically unproblematic:[5] it is not a little ironic that evangelicals so quickly and unapologetically give such credence to extra-biblical tradition when it suits us.

Contrastingly, there is only one apparent reference to mental illness in Scripture (Daniel 4), where Nebuchadnezzar loses and later regains his sanity in response to God's word of judgement – judgement which perhaps could be seen in parallel with the 'evil spirit for the Lord' that afflicts Saul (1 Samuel 16:14). It is remarkable that this reference occurs in Daniel, when the Persian influence on post-exilic Judaism was most pronounced, but it is equally remarkable that such a reference occurs anywhere in Scripture – the Bible as a whole seems ignorant of mental illness just as it is ignorant of epilepsy, of cancer, of kidney disease; in terms of medical science biblical passages clearly are rooted in particular cultural understandings.

But however the Bible may or may not understand mental illness, Jesus healed the sick and gave his disciples authority to do the same as marks of his coming kingdom (and the deliverance of men and women from demons, at very least, should be understood as an aspect of this general healing ministry). There are a few passages within the Gospels which could be interpreted in terms of Jesus healing 'all' who were sick,[6] similarly the narrative of Acts seems to suggest that all were healed who were touched by handkerchiefs and aprons that had been touched by Paul – though the text acknowledges that this was 'extraordinary' (Acts 19:11f.), but (even if this is the most appropriate way to interpret these references) generally there was something quite selective in the healing ministry of Jesus: there were probably several blind or lame beggars on the streets of Jericho and there were certainly others waiting to be healed by the pool of Bethesda. John's Gospel makes clear that the healing miracles of Jesus were 'signs' of his person and mission – a blind man receives his sight as a sign of deeper issues of sight and blindness and as a sign that Jesus himself is the light of the world; Lazarus is raised from the dead as a sign that Jesus himself is the resurrection and the life – and in the synoptic Gospels, though works of power and of compassion, miracles of healing are also signs of God's coming kingdom. But most significantly, every healing that is recorded in Scripture is provisional and limited: the blind, deaf, and lame that Jesus healed almost certainly later contracted some other malady from which they died; Jesus raised Lazarus from the dead, but Lazarus now is dead, as is every single person that Jesus healed (they may live to God but physically they're dead); Jesus commanded his disciples to heal the sick, raise the dead, and cast out demons, but all those disciples are dead, and while some of them were martyred some died, as most of us die, of 'something'. This life is not meant to be unending. This world and our lives within it are not yet as God ultimately chooses them to be. Sometimes miraculous healings still occur (though not infrequently such are partial and enigmatic) but most illnesses, now and then, remain unhealed. My best friend from my youth, despite many prayers, remains paralyzed. Despite much pleading I still live with recurrent depression. Despite asking three times, Paul was left with his thorn in the flesh, whatever it was. Perhaps, in the light of this provisionality and limitation, it is the healing of some rather than sickness itself that is problematic (why should this one be healed and not that one; why should healing be partial; why should healing be followed by death?). The focus of gospel proclamation is Jesus himself as the true definition of God and as the true definition of humanity. We distort the gospel (and thereby apostatize) when we shift its focus to ourselves, to our needs and desires, to our health, wealth, and well-being.

The purpose of this chapter, in anticipation of a sustained engagement with a psalm of lament, is to reflect on the very personal story of chapter one: how should we respond to mental illness or to any form of sickness and suffering? Our common assumption is that suffering of any kind is dissonant, a distortion of how things should be; we assume that sickness should be healed, that disability should be overcome – but might this understandable assumption itself be an unwitting distortion of the gospel?

Some time ago a former student contacted me. She and her husband (also a former student) have an autistic son and she wanted to discuss whether, in the resurrection, he would still be autistic – the difficulty being that, here and now, it is quite impossible to separate his autism from the person that he is. This may be less true of physical conditions (though it is not entirely untrue and the boundary between the physical and the mental is delusory) but it is a problematic distinction in most mental conditions.[7] I mentioned in the previous chapter that all but one of those interviewed by Stephen Fry in his two-part documentary did not wish to be other than they were. I'm sure this is incomprehensible to those peering in from the outside: who would want the despair of depression; who would want the embarrassment of mania? I would do anything to be rid of the numbing desolation of despair but I note in puzzlement that, while I can write rhymes at any time, I can only write poetry of any approximation to quality when I am depressed. And I have already confessed the difficulty (if not impossibility) of distinguishing mania from enthusiasm, obsession from fascination, being outrageous from being engaging. For all the pain of it, I would rather be as I am than live with the unremitting and boring greyness that was the experience of taking Lithium. As is true in so many aspects of life, that for which I am most grateful is inextricably bound up with that which I most regret and loathe. I would welcome healing if I could lose the despair without losing the insight and sensitivity, if I could lose the mania without losing the enthusiasm and passion. But since I'm not convinced that these things can be so easily distinguished, I'm not sure I want to be 'healed'; I would rather, with Paul, cling on to the promise that God's grace is sufficient in my weakness, and even that God is glorified in and through my weakness rather than by its removal. The one who is risen remains the one who was crucified; the glorified Jesus still bears the wounds of his crucifixion – maybe it is more appropriate to think of a future resurrection that transforms us than one that eradicates or abolishes the stories and distinctives that have shaped us.[8]

And, of course, I'm certainly not the first person to have wrestled with this condition (or any of its variations). The diagnosis of manic depression (or bi-polar disorder as it now is more commonly termed) is relatively recent but it is not hard or uncommon to look back at figures of history and ponder whether, had they been alive today, they would have be so labelled. What precisely was the 'black dog' with which Winston Churchill wrestled, and would his ancestor, John Churchill, have led the charge at Blenheim other than in manic recklessness? When you first are given this diagnosis it is reassuring to ponder the fact that others have suffered similarly and coped quite amazingly. And the history of the Church is littered with those who similarly have struggled and coped. Reflect for a moment on the depth of tortured angst that underlies the poetry of William Cowper. Not all that within Christian history that is termed the dark night of the soul had its roots in mental illness, but all who walked through that shadowed valley have wrestled similarly with despair and desolation.

Given the college in which I trained and in which I now teach it was especially poignant for me to discover that C. H. Spurgeon wrestled with periodic bouts of depression and occasionally had to take time out of pastoral ministry to recover. In an address included in a collection entitled *The Soul-Winner* he records an occasion when, in the depths of despair himself, he preached one evening on the opening verse of Psalm 22 before withdrawing for a while to his favourite retreat at Mentone in the south of France. In the service that evening, unbeknown to Spurgeon, was a man 'as nearly insane as he could be to be out of an asylum' who was so persuaded by the transparent reality out of which the preacher dealt with the text that he sought counsel from Spurgeon after the service and, on meeting him again some five years later, he confessed to Spurgeon that he had 'walked in the sunlight from that day till now'.[9] For Spurgeon, in late nineteenth-century England, to be as candid as he unfailingly was concerning his struggles with depression is remarkable – if there remains a stigma now concerning such conditions this was certainly the case then – yet Spurgeon admitted his weakness in writing and in public, to his students, to his colleagues, and to his congregation. It was reading of this incident, probably above all else, that convinced me early in my own journey to be similarly candid: 'we do not preach ourselves, but Jesus Christ as Lord, and ourselves as your servants for Jesus' sake' – but the servants that we are come with our thorns in the flesh, our weaknesses, our vulnerabilities (2 Corinthians 4:5).[10] The temptation to be less than honest in preaching and teaching is at least as great as the temptation to be self-focused – and avoiding the one while repudiating the other is less than easy to achieve. But if preachers, pastors, and teachers are not, like the apostle and like Spurgeon, open concerning their vulnerabilities, then by default they contribute to shallow and delusory triumphalisms which, now as then, threaten to distort the Christian message and discredit the Church. You rarely lose credibility by admitting weakness – you invariably lose credibility by not admitting weakness when that weakness is apparent to all. As I intimated in the Introduction to this book, being candid about depression has sometimes led me into encounters that I did not (and perhaps could not) handle effectively and appropriately, but the alternative is deception and self-deception. The lesson to be learnt (by painful experience) is that one form of vulnerability can lead all too easily to another and that, while the first may be irremediable, the second is avoidable.

If it is foolish and anachronistic to apply contemporary psychiatric diagnoses to figures of the past it is similarly foolish to apply such to characters narrated in Scripture or to the biblical writers themselves. In the latter case, especially with respect to the psalmists, the issue is considerably compounded by the liberal use of metaphor (this will be discussed to some degree in the next chapter). It simply is not always possible to discern the precise nature of the problem of which the psalmist complains, less still the manner of sickness which may be suffered. But clearly, time and again, these writers were suffering from something; they were vulnerable; they were threatened; they were fearful. And quite often they were angry, angry not just about their circumstances, but angry with God for seeming to allow such circumstances, angry with God for seeming to abandon them to such circumstances. The Bible is not short on candour (though our familiarity and falsely pious reading can obscure this candour). Over and again psalmists and prophets complain to God. Just as 2 Corinthians offers some sustained insight into what it felt like to be an apostle, so the Book of Jeremiah offers sustained insight into what it felt like to be a prophet – and it wasn't a bundle of fun:

> Why is my pain unending
>   and my wound grievous and incurable?
> Will you be to me like a deceptive brook,
>   like a spring that fails? (Jeremiah 15:18).

These questions can just as easily be translated as statements: the pain is unending and the wound is incurable; God has been like a dried-up spring; Jeremiah turned up and God wasn't there. God calls the prophet to repent but he never rebukes the honesty – indeed, the ubiquity of such honesty in Scripture sanctions it and sanctifies it. Without such honesty God cannot begin to work with us or within us in a way that is glorifying. Scripture offers no encouragement for pious platitudes and self-deception – God is never deceived.

Most famously, of course, Job complains to God. He never curses God but he certainly curses the day that he was born and he despairs of his own situation and of the theologically informed but spiritually vacuous counsel of his friends. Job is not an easy book to categorize or comprehend. Perhaps we should view it as a very long and dramatized psalm of lament with the opening two chapters serving as an extended super-scription. Perhaps, most significantly, we should notice that neither Job nor his friends are ever given the (admittedly strange and problematic) information that we are given in these opening chapters: Job has no sense of being in the hands of Satan (however we understand Satan in the context of this book); as far as Job is concerned, he is in the hands of God – this is the essence of his problem and the basis of his complaint, but it is also the source of his hope, a hope that emerges even from the darkest depths of despair. The deepest problem in the book of Job seems to hinge on the question 'why? – Job's friends are quick to offer explanations for his suffering but, for Job, no explanation is satisfying. Nor does the book, even in its climax and conclusion, offer an answer (the dialogue between Satan and God with which the narrative began is never revisited). When God speaks to Job out of the whirlwind it is not to offer satisfactory explanation but to remind Job of the limits of his understanding.[11] It is tempting (and not at all uncommon) to conclude that it is the mere presence and speaking of God that is sufficient for Job, no matter what God actually says – but (uncommonly perhaps) it was never the absence of God that was Job's expressed problem, on the contrary, he longed for God's absence, for God to turn away from him and from whatever sins he may have committed and to leave him alone:

> What are human beings that you make so much of them,
>   that you give them so much attention,
> that you examine them every morning
>   and test them every moment?
> Will you never look away from me,
>   or let me alone even for an instant?
> If I have sinned, what have I done to you,
>   O you who watch over us all?
> Why have you made me your target?
> Have I become a burden to you?
> Why do you not pardon my offences
>   and forgive my sins?
> For I shall soon lie down in the dust;
>   you will search for me, but I shall be no more. (Job 7:17–21).

In this respect Job would seem to be unusual: for Jeremiah, for the psalmists, and for countless Christians over the centuries, it is the felt absence of God rather than any threatening presence that is the most profound aspect and root of despair – and here (finally) we arrive at the purpose and focus of this book. In the previous chapter I listed some of the symptoms of depression (albeit, and inevitably, personal symptoms), but the most distressing symptom of all was deliberately omitted from that list. Generally speaking (and I do not want to over-generalize), one of the first signs of depression is the loss of any sense of spiritual feeling or presence, not a feeling of dread but a feeling of numbness and emptiness, the sense that prayers are projected into nothingness and therefore pointless, the feeling of being abandoned. I was continually bemused by the irony that, as pastor of a lively charismatic church, I could pass months in spiritual numbness, devoid of any felt spiritual experience. It is the crushing darkness of this sense of God's apparent absence that is the most distressing aspect of clinical depression for the Christian. And, whether rooted in clinical depression or not, it is this sense of spiritual numbness, of being deserted by God, that constitutes the so-called dark night of the soul. And whether rooted in clinical depression or not, this spiritual darkness has afflicted countless Christians throughout Christian history. Many have reflected on it (which is how we know they suffered it). Many more (I suspect) endured in silence. A year ago the press reported letters of the late Mother Teresa that confessed a deep questioning of faith and a sense of separation from God beginning soon after the commencement of her work in Calcutta and continuing thereafter, from the late 1940s until her death in 1997: 'I am told God loves me and yet the reality of darkness and coldness and emptiness is so great that nothing touches my soul'.[12] Or consider the following extract from a letter by John Wesley to Charles, his brother:

> In one of [my] last [I] was saying [I] do not feel the wrath of God abiding on [me]; nor can I believe it does. And yet (this is the mystery) [I do not love God. I never did.] Therefore [I never] *believed* in the Christian sense of the word. Therefore [I am only an] honest heathen, a proselyte of the Temple, one of the φοβούμενοι τὸν θεόν. [Those that fear God.] And yet to be so employed of God! and so hedged in that I can neither get forward nor backward! Surely there

never was such an instance before, from the beginning of the world. If I [ever have had] *that faith,* it would not be so strange. But I never had any other ἔλεγχος [proof] of the eternal or invisible world than [I have] now; and that is [none at all], unless such as fairly shines from reason's glimmering ray. [I have no] *direct* witness, I do not say that [I am a child of God], but of anything invisible or eternal.

And yet I dare not preach otherwise than I do, either concerning faith, or love, or justification or perfection. And yet I find rather an increase than a decrease of zeal for the whole work of God and every part of it. I am φερόμενος [borne along], I know not how, that I can't stand still. I want all the world to come to ὃν οὐκ οἶδα [what I do not know]. Neither am I impelled to this by fear of any kind. I have no more fear than love. Or if I have [any fear, it is not that of falling] into hell but of falling into nothing.[13]

Now if this letter had been written before the Aldersgate experience in 1738, perhaps from Georgia, we should not find it so surprising, but it is dated 1766, when Wesley's ministry was at its height, but when, as the letter reveals, he was nevertheless struggling with a lack of faith, a lack of any felt assurance, a lack of felt presence. But maybe we should not find this letter surprising at all. Maybe we should recognize that this sense of darkness and forsakenness is common, not least amongst those who publicly are active in Christian ministry.

And here also for me, both in the experience of such witnesses and in the prayers which are the psalms, was a primary source of reassurance: not only was I not alone in experiencing depression and self-loathing, I was not alone in this sense of God-forsakenness, in the loss of any sense of felt spiritual experience, even in a loss of faith. Hymns remembered from my youth became more deeply meaningful, became means through which I could express my own fears and doubt. Both Job and the psalms of lament came to prominence in my reading of Scripture, not as fuel for depressive wallowing but simply again as means of expressing what I wanted and needed to say but could not say for myself. Surprisingly (and perhaps unusually) for a Baptist, the ancient liturgy and prayers of the Church became means through which I could worship and pray when any personal sense of worship or ability to pray had fled. And, maybe most significantly, the sacraments of the Church took on a deeper significance as promises and seals of that which I could not feel or experience. Whether or not I felt a child of God, I was baptised. Whether or not I still felt called by God, I was ordained. Whether or not I felt the presence of God, the bread and wine of Holy Communion were signs and seals of the presence of Christ and of my forgiveness and participation in him. My lack of felt presence, even my lack of felt faith, could not nullify the promise that was sacramentally sealed. And in this way and by these ordained means, even a sense of unremitting darkness and absence can, paradoxically, become a place of promised presence. I may lack any sense of feeling, I may struggle to believe at all, I may be convinced only of my wretchedness, I may feel abandoned by God, but the promise of his sacramental presence, not bounded by my feelings or lack of feelings, remains.

I mentioned in the last chapter a period of about two months in 1974 when Rosie and I stayed with a deacon and his wife from the Baptist church in Maldon. In an earlier book on sacramental theology I recount an incident that occurred towards the end of that time and I can do no better than to end this chapter by recounting it again.[14] I must have been improving in health since the couple with whom we were staying, together with Rosie, had gone to the evening service and left me minding their two small children. That service had been a service of Holy Communion and, on their return, they determined that (however I might feel about it) I should share in communion with them. Bread and (very good) wine were placed on their coffee table, we all knelt together, and I recited words of institution (this, after all, was my 'job'). I really cannot remember the degree of hypocrisy that I felt at the time in doing this, but I do remember what I didn't feel – I felt no sense of God's presence, I felt nothing whatsoever, if I retained any sense of personal faith it was, by then, the merest glimmer. Yet, as we knelt at that table, the thought (rather than feeling) came to me that, just as the bread and wine were simply there on the table, whatever my feelings or even my faith, so once in history Christ had suffered on the Cross and here, by means of the bread and wine, his body and blood were present for me as surely as the bread and wine were present, without prejudice to my lack of feeling or even my lack of faith but solely by virtue of God's promise. I have no prejudice against felt experience and, in happier times, I have experienced charismatic phenomena, but this experience – entirely devoid of any felt experience – remains the most profound and formative experience of my Christian life. That evening I came to understand the meaning of grace in a way that I had never understood it previously. In utter darkness, in the absence of all felt presence, promise remains.

Dear Lord,
you promised never to leave us or forsake us:
so where are you?
I cry to you morning and evening;
I lie awake at night;
I sink myself in daily routine –
but there is no answer;
no sense of your presence;
no relief.
I deserve nothing from you,
but I have your promise,
your gracious promise to be with me,
even in the darkness.
So where are you?
Please grant me some sign of your presence,
even if the darkness remains.
For the sake of Jesus Christ, your Son,
who promises to nourish us through bread and wine
with his own body and blood.
Amen.

Chapter Three

Darkness and the Psalmist

For the director of music.
To [the tune of] "The Doe of the Morning."
A psalm of David.

My God, my God, why have you forsaken me?
　　Why are you so far from saving me,
　　so far from the words of my groaning?
O my God, I cry out by day, but you do not answer,
　　by night, and am not silent.
Yet you are enthroned as the Holy One;
　　you are the praise of Israel.[1]
In you our ancestors put their trust;
　　they trusted and you delivered them.
They cried to you and were saved;
　　in you they trusted and were not disappointed.
But I am a worm and not a human being,
　　scorned by everyone and despised by the people.
All who see me mock me;
　　they hurl insults, shaking their heads:
"He trusts in the LORD?
　　let the LORD rescue him.
Let him deliver him,
　　since he delights in him."
Yet you brought me out of the womb;
　　you made me trust in you
　　even at my mother's breast.

From birth I was cast upon you;
  from my mother's womb you have been my God.
Do not be far from me,
  for trouble is near
  and there is no one to help.
Many bulls surround me;
  strong bulls of Bashan encircle me.
Roaring lions tearing their prey
  open their mouths wide against me.
I am poured out like water,
  and all my bones are out of joint.
My heart has turned to wax;
  it has melted away within me.
My strength is dried up like a potsherd,
  and my tongue sticks to the roof of my mouth;
  you lay me[2] in the dust of death.
Dogs have surrounded me;
  a band of evil people has encircled me,
  they have pierced[3] my hands and my feet.
I can count all my bones;
  people stare and gloat over me.
They divide my garments among them
  and cast lots for my clothing.
But you, O LORD, be not far off;
  O my Strength, come quickly to help me.
Deliver my life from the sword,
  my precious life from the power of the dogs.
Rescue me from the mouth of the lions;
  Save[4] me from the horns of the wild oxen.
I will declare your name to my people;
  in the congregation I will praise you.
You who fear the LORD, praise him!
  All you descendants of Jacob, honour him!
  Revere him, all you descendants of Israel!
For he has not despised or disdained
  the suffering of the afflicted one;
he has not hidden his face from him

but has listened to his cry for help.
From you comes the theme of my praise in the great assembly;
    before those who fear you[5] will I fulfil my vows.
The poor will eat and be satisfied;
    they who seek the LORD will praise him—
    may your hearts live forever!
All the ends of the earth
    will remember and turn to the LORD,
and all the families of the nations
    will bow down before him,
for dominion belongs to the LORD
    and he rules over the nations.
All the rich of the earth will feast and worship;
    all who go down to the dust will kneel before him—
    those who cannot keep themselves alive.
Posterity will serve him;
future generations will be told about the Lord.
They will proclaim his righteousness
    to a people yet unborn—
    for he has done it. (Psalm 22)

On the basis that I probably would never again have the opportunity to get to grips with Hebrew and Greek (I had been taught Latin at school – I only wish I had learnt more diligently), as a student I opted for as many papers on the Hebrew and Greek text of Scripture as the University of London regulations then permitted. There was a standard Old Testament paper, with Hebrew passages from 2 Kings and Psalms, and there was an Old Testament theology paper, with passages chosen from a wide selection of Old Testament books for their particular theological pertinence. Psalm 22 was one of these theologically pertinent passages (though I have never really understood the basis on which it was included in the selection). Consequently, during those years as a theological student when recurrent depression was beginning to take a hold of my life, I spent much time reading and studying this psalm, wrestling with the Hebrew text and with the variations between manuscripts, translations, and citations, and wrestling more profoundly with its theological and personal significance. There is much in the psalm which is obscure – it is rich in metaphor though the reference of these metaphors is no longer clear to us – but its opening cry of despair connects immediately and the manner in which that despair is expressed and compounded, notwithstanding the obscurity of metaphor, was (and is) similarly personally descriptive and defining.

For the director of music.
To [the tune of] "The Doe of the Morning."
A psalm of David.

Perhaps the first thing to say about the psalm is that we know so little about it, its author, or its occasion. Tradition has understood the superscription לדוד (*l^edavid*) as signifying Davidic authorship but the Hebrew prefix is more simply translated as 'to David' or 'for David' and may be no more than a standard formula for identifying a royal psalm, a poem dedicated to one of the kings of Judah. While some might presume to deduce from the language of the psalm that it originates from a particular period of Israel's history such constructions are tentative and contestable. We simply do not know who wrote this psalm or under what particular circumstances it was written or (as we will explore in the next chapter) the precise place it held within Israel's worship. Even if David were to be presumed to be its author, there is no clue within the psalm that would help us to connect its occasion to any specific incident or circumstance within David's life as it is narrated in Samuel and Chronicles – there are several incidents recorded in David's life when he was in distress but the richness (or strangeness) of the metaphors employed in the psalm militates against any (probably misguided) attempt to determine an occasion for the psalm in David's life. All that we really know of the psalm – to state the blindingly obvious – is that someone wrote it and that someone, whoever they were, wrote it out of a sense of crisis, out of a sense of worthlessness, out of a sense of being deserted by God. There may be much that we don't know about the psalm, there may be much of its imagery that eludes us, but nonetheless we should take with absolute seriousness that which we do know: we should assume that this unknown author writes with honesty and integrity; we should accept the candour of the psalm at face value.

> My God, my God, why have you forsaken me?
>   Why are you so far from saving me,
>   so far from the words of my groaning?
> O my God, I cry out by day, but you do not answer,
>   by night, and am not silent.

For the Church, of course, that the opening words of the psalm are spoken by Jesus on the Cross has massively influenced the manner in which the psalm has been heard and even translated. That Jesus speaks these words of desolation, whether he is quoting from the psalm or not, can dull the psalm's immediacy, can sever it from the particular though general sense of desolation in the experience of the psalmist and in our experience for the sake of the particular and unique sense of desolation in the Cross of Christ; I come to hear the psalm as expressive of Christ's feeling of abandonment rather than as expressive of the psalmist's feeling of abandonment and my feeling of abandonment. Moreover, the reference within the psalm to the dividing of garments and the casting of lots for clothing (v.18), especially as this is taken up in some later manuscripts of Matthew's gospel and in John 19:24 (though John's gospel makes no reference to this cry of dereliction), serves to reinforce a reading of the psalm specifically with reference to Christ. That the Septuagint speaks of 'piercing'[6] in verse sixteen (rather than a 'lion')[7] further strengthens the association with Christ's crucifixion and is followed by many English translations.

Perhaps this is a convenient point to comment more generally on the use of metaphor within this psalm (as within so many psalms).[8] English translators can perhaps be excused for referring to the piercing of hands and feet through the sheer oddness of the encircling evil people, previously likened to dogs, now likened to a lion at the psalmist's hands and feet. And when the psalmist has previously spoken of being surrounded by bulls of Bashan (v.12), of roaring lions opening their mouths (v.13), when there is a plea to be rescued from the mouths of lions and the horns of wild oxen (v.21), one can be forgiven for wondering whether the psalmist has fallen into some primitive menagerie or safari park. And what does it mean to be 'poured out like water', for bones to be 'out of joint', for a heart to 'turn to wax', and for a heart to melt away (v.14)? What is a 'potsherd' and how does this illustrate the drying up of strength (v.15)? This imagery is foreign to us (and the problem is not simply one of translation).[9] While I suppose this could all be 'literal' language (the psalmist could have wandered into a safari park) this surely is highly unlikely. In all probability what we have here are graphic metaphors for extreme physical and emotional suffering – we cannot now specify the significance of the metaphors or identify the particular nature of the suffering, but we can be persuaded of the gravity of that suffering and of the psalmist's distress. And whatever else we do, we must resist the temptation to dwell on those metaphors that can be read as prefiguring Christ's crucifixion at the expense of those metaphors which don't fit so readily; we must resist the temptation to focus on the gravity of Christ's distress without also and firstly focusing on the psalmist's distress (and thereby enabling an expression of our own more common distress).

Here then is one who, through circumstances which now we have no hope of identifying, calls out to God by day and by night, but with no response; one whose groaning seems pointless; one who feels deserted and abandoned. And it is this sense of abandonment by God which seemingly poses an even deeper and more devastating problem for the psalmist than the circumstances (whatever those circumstances may be) that gave rise to the distress in the first place. The psalmist's expressed problem is not 'why has this happened to me?' but 'why have you forsaken me?'.[10] We should not for a single moment minimize the gravity of the psalmist's perceived circumstances: we might not now be able to relate to the metaphors employed in the psalm but it is reasonable to conclude that they signify extreme distress in response to affliction that was personal, physical, and emotional. Yet the dominant distress of the psalm is identified in its opening – not distress at these circumstances but distress at the perceived absence of God. For anyone who truly knows God, I suspect this will always be the case. For the one who knows God not at all or who actively disbelieves in God, the focus of distress will inevitably rest on the circumstances themselves (though many who spend their lives ignoring God are eager enough to resort to blaming God when some form of disaster strikes). For those who, like Job, know and honour God – and for many who make no profession to know God – the question 'why' is virtually unavoidable. Why should this be happening to me or to those that I most dearly love? What have I done to deserve this (though for many of us the more honest question would be 'what I have done not to deserve this?')? If God is all-powerful and all-loving why is he allowing this to happen? As we noted in the last chapter, this was Job's question and it is a question that recurs throughout human history and not infrequently, I suspect, in our own lives. But it is not the primary question for this psalmist: when in the face of opposition, oppression, and suffering God seems to be absent, it is this felt absence – rather than the opposition, oppression, and suffering itself – that, for the one who truly knows God, constitutes the most profound distress. The personal and most pressing question is not whether an all-powerful and all-loving God would allow these circumstances but rather whether an all-powerful and all-loving God would abandon me to these circumstances. I might be kidding myself, but I would like to think that I could endure the valley of the shadow of death – or any other physical or emotional threat – if I knew that the divine shepherd was with me, to comfort and guide me, but I dread that or any other valley of darkness without that presence and comfort. Those who know God and have ever experienced any felt sense of the absence of God will not need me to belabour the point. Whoever this psalmist was and whatever specific circumstances this psalmist faced, it is this horror of abandonment by God that prompts the psalm.

> Yet you are enthroned as the Holy One;
> > you are the praise of Israel.[11]
> In you our ancestors put their trust;
> > they trusted and you delivered them.
> They cried to you and were saved;
> > in you they trusted and were not disappointed.
> But I am a worm and not a human being,
> > scorned by everyone and despised by the people.
> All who see me mock me;
> > they hurl insults, shaking their heads:
> "He trusts in the LORD?
> > let the LORD rescue him.
> Let him deliver him,
> > since he delights in him."

In this English translation the word 'yet' occurs twice in the first part of the psalm and the first time it occurs it is qualified by the word 'but'.[12] Once again, those who have experienced a sense of the felt absence of God will recognize the internal arguments that ensue. In the first place there is an appeal to history, to the recorded experience of Israel, to the recorded experience of the Church. Scripture and tradition testify to the faithfulness of God; the story of God's people throughout history, reinforced by innumerable pious biographies and autobiographies, testify to the trustworthiness of God – in the past God has heard and in the past God has acted; our spiritual ancestors were never disappointed by this God. But, for the psalmist, this form of reassurance is not reassuring: 'I am a worm and not a human being'. The objection seems a little extreme: a proper humility is one thing but apparent self-loathing is something else. We want to rebuke the psalmist, perhaps we could commend the psalmist to a good Christian counsellor who can address issues of self-image. Everything within us wants to protest that the psalmist is not a worm, that the psalmist is a human being, that the psalmist is truly an heir of those who, in the past, have trusted God and have not been disappointed. But it is to no avail. The psalmist has good reason for this impoverished self-image. From the psalmist's perspective, this impoverished self-image has been reinforced over and again. It now becomes clear that it is not just God who seems to have rejected the psalmist but that all who see the psalmist revile, mock, and abuse the psalmist; their mocking reinforces the perception that the psalmist is trusting God in vain. This language of mocking, of course, resonates again with Christ's crucifixion – but here too we must not allow this understandable resonance to distract us from the fact that many others, before and since Christ, have been mocked and rejected by their contemporaries.

We should note also that which the psalm does not specify. There are psalms of lament which are also psalms of confession, but this is not one of them. Particular models for interpreting the atonement and, thereby, for interpreting Christ's cry of dereliction (interpretations which we will ponder in Chapter Six of this book) tend to prejudice our reading of this psalm, prompting us to assume that the psalmist is a worm because the psalmist is a sinner and that it is sin and the consciousness of sin that has separated the psalmist from God. But, in its Hebrew text at least, the psalm makes no mention of sin whatsoever. The Septuagint translates the second line of the opening verse as '. . . the words of my transgressions are far from my salvation'[13] – apart from this unlikely inference, the Psalm lacks any explicit mention of sin or sinfulness. The assumption that the psalmist identifies as a worm because the psalmist is a sinner is precisely that, an assumption, an assumption that is without any clear warrant in the Hebrew text of the psalm. In distinction to the book of Job and to some other psalms of lament there is no explicit protestation of innocence here but neither is there any explicit consciousness of sin. Certainly, on the basis of the connectedness of this psalm within the canon of Holy Scripture, we should affirm that 'all have sinned and fall short of the glory of God' (Romans 3:23); certainly we should affirm that the whole of creation is 'groaning' and that creation's present frustration is somehow linked to human sinfulness (Romans 8:19ff.); but it is a frightful and inexcusable error to assume that every particular instance of suffering or frustration is an outcome of specific sin. Job, in the midst of appalling suffering and in conflict with the judgemental theological assumptions of his friends, maintains his 'innocence' before God and is ultimately vindicated by God; Job's suffering specifically was not an outcome of his sin. And neither is there any persuasive reason to suppose that the suffering of this psalmist, or this despairing sense of forsakenness, is specifically the outcome of sin. This world is not how God ultimately desires it to be, and we within it are not yet how God desires us to be, and, here and now, the world is characterized by appalling cruelty, suffering, and pain – and sometimes too, without prejudice to any specific sin, by a sense of being forsaken by God. The psalmist's self-identification as a worm may signify a sense of sinfulness but this is not necessarily the case: not all wretchedness and self-loathing issues from a consciousness of sin; not every guilty conscience is entirely justified; a sense of wretchedness and of guilt can be symptoms of sickness; a sense of wretchedness and guilt can be prompted by the extremities of human rejection.

> Yet you brought me out of the womb;
>> you made me trust in you
>> even at my mother's breast.
> From birth I was cast upon you;
>> from my mother's womb you have been my God.
> Do not be far from me,
>> for trouble is near
>> and there is no one to help.

Both in the Hebrew text and in the Septuagint this second 'yet' translates a much stronger conjunction, often translated by our words 'because' or 'for',[14] and possibly suggests a stronger link with the previous verse: the psalmist trusts in God because God brought the psalmist from the womb; God brought the psalmist to such trust. The appeal to history and tradition, to the experience of our ancestors, seems to have been entirely ineffective, but this more personal appeal to personal history issues in renewed prayer – it doesn't issue in any assurance of God's presence that would be the answer to prayer and the relieving of desolation (if remembrance of personal experience relieved this sense of desolation the prayer would not need to be repeated); but it does issue in renewed prayer rather than a repeated expression of wretchedness and worthlessness.

I write as a Baptist yet I concede (reluctantly) that I have no memory of ever having not trusted in God (and, if Baptism is properly the Baptism of 'Believers', who is to determine the inception of genuine faith in the life of a child?).[15] As I've mentioned already, I was born into a devout Christian home, I was taught to pray as a child, I was taught to love Scripture as a child, and I can never remember not believing that there was a God who loved me and who sent his Son to save me. Throughout my adult life there have been many times when I have felt little sense of God's presence but though, as I grow older, there is an expanding range of biblical, theological, and philosophical issues that I confess I do not understand, I think I would find it impossible to disbelieve in God (questions of the mere existence of physical reality, the nature of eternity and infinity, and the sense of purposefulness that underlies ethics – all resist alternative explanations) but, far more fundamentally, in the light of the narrative of the gospel, a narrative echoed over and again in my life (and in the lives of those close to me), I would find it impossible to disbelieve that this God loves me. This, in a sense, is the problem: if I didn't believe in God, if I didn't believe the gospel story, if the narrative of my life and the lives of those I love didn't confirm that gospel story, then there would be no basis for the despair of God-forsakenness, there would merely be the nihilistic despair of nothingness, of pointlessness, of hopelessness. That Job continued to believe that he was in God's hands was the source of his deepest problem, but it was also the source of his continuing hope. It is precisely because I have been brought all my life to trust God that the sense of being shut-off from God is the bleakest and most troubling aspect of clinical depression. The psalmist has known God from birth, every experience of life has brought the psalmist to trust God, this is the source of the distress that arises from the sense of God-forsakenness, but it is the remembrance of this personal history that issues in renewed prayer that God will not remain distant, that God will hear and answer and act for the psalmist's deliverance.[16]

Many bulls surround me;
    strong bulls of Bashan encircle me.
Roaring lions tearing their prey
    open their mouths wide against me.
I am poured out like water,
    and all my bones are out of joint.
My heart has turned to wax;
    it has melted away within me.
My strength is dried up like a potsherd,
    and my tongue sticks to the roof of my mouth;
    you lay me in the dust of death.
Dogs have surrounded me;
    a band of evil people has encircled me,
    they have pierced my hands and my feet.
I can count all my bones;
    people stare and gloat over me.
They divide my garments among them
    and cast lots for my clothing.
But you, O LORD, be not far off;
    O my Strength, come quickly to help me.
Deliver my life from the sword,
    my precious life from the power of the dogs.
Rescue me from the mouth of the lions;
    save me from the horns of the wild oxen.

I have already commented on the problematic nature of the metaphors of this psalm, of the common Christian tendency to focus on those metaphors that can be interpreted in relation to Christ's crucifixion, of the inaccessibility of this graphic imagery.

But we can confidently assume that this graphic imagery, so foreign and unnatural to us, would not have been strange or foreign to the psalmist or to the psalmist's immediate readers. Words do not have an inherent and fixed meaning: if the meaning (or significance) of words is 'fixed' in any sense it is as an outcome of common usage within a community of communication, a community that commonly employs those words. That I am writing these words while sitting on a chair, next to a table, and occasionally looking out of the window, rather than sitting on my *Stuhl*, next to a *Tisch*, looking out of a *Fenster* indicates that I inhabit a community that communicates in English rather than German. There is nothing inherent in the word 'window' or the word *'Fenster'* to signify a pane of glass, set in a frame, set in a wall, through which one can see what is outside of the house – that words 'mean' is simply a convention of language. And that I can refer to a mob as 'a pack of hungry wolves', that William Wordsworth can refer to daffodils 'dancing', are also meaningful within a community of communication: daffodils don't dance and human beings are a different species to wolves, but the words signify something within a community that can grasp the reference – indeed, metaphorical language, though it is vulnerable to misunderstanding, has the potential to convey significance that could not be conveyed so effectively by more literal language. Winston Churchill referred to depression as 'black dog' – I don't know whether anyone had employed this metaphor before, but it communicates in two words what otherwise it might take a paragraph to convey. Metaphor conveys more rather than less but it only conveys anything at all if readers and hearers can follow the track of thought to what is being signified. I think I know what the psalmist means by speaking of those who are threatening him as 'dogs' or as 'lions' (though I'm less sure of what is intended by 'bulls' and 'oxen'), I think I might understand what the psalmist is intending by speaking of being 'poured out like water' or a heart melting away within – but I might be mistaken in my inferences and I certainly have no way of knowing (even if the psalmist's more immediate readers had any way of knowing) the precise circumstances to which the psalmist is responding. I may not understand these metaphors but I understand them sufficiently to realize that they signify great distress and desperation. And I understand fully that, in these circumstances whatever their precise nature, the psalmist longs for God not to remain distant.

> I will declare your name to my people;
>> in the congregation I will praise you.
> You who fear the LORD, praise him!
>> All you descendants of Jacob, honour him!
>> Revere him, all you descendants of Israel!
> For he has not despised or disdained
>> the suffering of the afflicted one;
> he has not hidden his face from him
>> but has listened to his cry for help.
> From you comes the theme of my praise in the great assembly;
>> before those who fear you will I fulfil my vows.

What happened? It's certainly tempting to think that something has happened, so marked is the change of tone within the psalm – and, as we will see in the next chapter, Old Testament scholarship has not been lacking in plausible theories concerning the significance of this change of tone, at least within the liturgy of the people of Israel. Perhaps some priest or some angelic mediator came to reassure the psalmist of God's presence even in the continuing context of suffering and oppression. Perhaps the suffering and oppression – whatever it may have been – was relieved or in some way brought to an end, bringing the psalmist to conclude that God, though apparently absent and silent, had in reality been present, had heard the psalmist's prayer, and had brought about this deliverance. Such are possibilities which cannot be discounted but the psalm itself makes no mention of them. They are speculative inferences, perhaps quite reasonable inferences, perhaps inferences prompted by the structure of other psalms of this genre, but inferences nonetheless and, as will be reiterated in subsequent chapters, our proper response must be to the text of Scripture itself rather than to what may or may not lie behind the text as we have received it. And the text itself makes no mention of any deliverance or mediated reassurance. All that the text offers is this abrupt and explicitly unexplained change of tone and mood – and we are invited to hear and to respond to this change of mood without any explanation, without any presumed change of circumstance. As the psalm presently stands it is precisely the one who is opposed and oppressed who declares God's praise; the one who considers himself a 'worm' who now declares that his suffering is neither despised nor disdained by God; the one who deems himself forsaken who now declares that God has 'listened to his cry for help' and 'has not hidden his face from him'. If any change has occurred we are not told of it and, in the absence of such a reference, perhaps we should rather assume that no change has occurred whatsoever; the oppression and suffering persist; the sense of forsakenness remains; such constitute the continuing context in which this change of tone occurs.[17]

Perhaps the more searching and disconcerting question we should pose to ourselves is that of why we are so deeply predisposed to assume that some change in circumstance has occurred, to assume (correspondingly) that without any change of circumstance this change of tone is implausible? As the psalm stands, without speculating about transforming events which may or may not lie behind it, it offers a personal and public confession of confidence precisely in the context of oppression, despair, and forsakenness. Perhaps it is the possibility of such a confession within such a context that constitutes the most profound significance of the psalm? Perhaps the psalm has more to teach us about the nature of faith and the relationship between faith and perception than about theodicy, than about the problem of suffering and forsakenness in itself?

Let's assume that nothing has changed (and the text itself gives us no warrant to assume otherwise). Let's assume that the psalmist is still surrounded by a metaphorical menagerie of oppression. Let's assume the psalmist still feels abandoned to this oppression, forsaken by God. What we then have in this change of tone is a confession of faith despite the circumstances, a faith that is confessed over and above perception and feelings. And maybe this is significant of the nature of authentic faith – or, at least, the nature of the faith of this psalmist and of so many others we encounter in Scripture. Our contemporary tendency is to relate faith to tangible (and usually immediate) outcomes, to illuminating insight, and to a feeling of confidence and assurance – I feel confident and assured, therefore I have faith. The flaw in these assumptions, of course, is that for quite a lot of the time I feel neither confident nor assured, I have little or no understanding of what is happening to me or why it is happening, and I certainly lack any immediate or tangible outcome to my prayers. That which the psalm has to teach us, therefore, is that a lack of feeling, a lack of understanding, or a lack of immediate resolution, need not imply a corresponding lack of faith. And, if faith is understood in this way, as an assured knowledge rather than a feeling of assurance, then this sudden change of tone and confession of faith should not surprise us – faith in this sense has characterized the psalm from its beginning; the cry of desolation, inasmuch as it is a cry to God, is itself an appeal of faith; the recitation of God's faithfulness in Israel's history is a confession of faith; most particularly, the recalling of being in God's hands from birth is a confession of faith – faith is not a feeling, it is without prejudice to feeling; faith is confidence in God over and against circumstance, understanding, and feeling; faith declares what feeling doubts and circumstance denies; faith affirms God's nature and faithfulness even when God is felt to be absent.

There may be many valid ways of hearing this psalm, many scholarly possibilities of locating its dramatic form within the liturgy of ancient Israel, many more personal and devotional possibilities for receiving comfort through these verses. This is intended as an unashamedly personal response to the psalm, an invitation to hear it as I have heard it – and this is how I have heard it, both in encouragement and sometimes in rebuke, when circumstances have appeared bleak, when God has seemed to be distant, when I haven't had a clue what was going on, when despair was overwhelming. All such feelings and contexts are irrelevant to authentic faith. Confident trust in God is grounded in his revealed nature and is without prejudice to feeling, insight, or circumstance. The psalmist can affirm God's covenant faithfulness without the feeling of such. The psalmist can affirm God's deliverance without immediate evidence of such. The psalmist can do this on the basis of the faith of Israel that has been his own personal confidence. The psalmist can do this on the basis of God's revelation in history and in his own personal life. And in the light of the Cross and resurrection of Christ, understood at least partly in response to this psalm, we have a more profound basis for such trust than this psalmist could have conceived.

> The poor will eat and be satisfied;
>   they who seek the LORD will praise him—
>   may your hearts live forever!
> All the ends of the earth
>   will remember and turn to the LORD,
> and all the families of the nations
>   will bow down before him,
> for dominion belongs to the LORD
>   and he rules over the nations.
> All the rich of the earth will feast and worship;
>   all who go down to the dust will kneel before him—
>   those who cannot keep themselves alive.
> Posterity will serve him;
> future generations will be told about the Lord.
> They will proclaim his righteousness
>   to a people yet unborn—
> for he has done it.

While some other possibilities for interpreting this psalm in the context of Israel's worship will be considered in the next chapter, it is worth noting at this point that, though this is an intensely personal psalm, it concludes in a wholly non-individualistic way. In actuality, of course, the psalm (though intensely personal) was never individualistic: the faith confessed is the faith of Israel just as the sense of desolation was compounded if not rooted in a communal rejection and oppression. Nor is this concluding section impersonal or detached: the unequivocal confidence the psalmist expresses is rooted in all that has gone before and is as much a personal confession of faith as the immediately preceding verses. But it is a universal hope, stretching beyond the boundaries of Israel to the 'ends of the earth' and to 'all the families of the nations'; stretching beyond the psalmist's present to 'future generations' who, in their own time, will 'be told about the Lord' and who, consequently, will themselves 'proclaim his righteousness'. Moreover, it is a universal hope that supersedes any apparent blessing or rejection, that embraces both the 'rich of the earth' and those who 'go down to the dust', those who 'cannot keep themselves alive'. A universal hope need not imply a universal salvation – the Hebrew word here translated 'remember' (זכר) has covenant connotations and issues in a turning to the Lord and a bowing down before him – but no qualification should detract from the extraordinary scope of the psalmist's hope. The Old Testament with a single voice identifies Israel as God's chosen people, but over and again the Old Testament attests this election as for the blessing of all nations, for the blessing of the earth itself. Divine election cannot be merely a private or individualistic affair anymore than can divine deliverance. The confidence the psalmist confesses concerning his own deliverance as an outcome of God's faithfulness, notwithstanding continuing oppression and persisting despair, must reverberate in an all-embracing confidence issuing from an unqualified divine faithfulness – even if that confidence is expressed in the face of present contradictory realities.

In Old Testament Hebrew there are but two tenses: a perfect tense signifying completed action and an imperfect tense signifying continuing or uncompleted action. The final word of this psalm is in the perfect tense, 'he has done it' (עשׂה), an action has been completed – yet clearly this universal hope (as also, I suspect, the personal deliverance of the psalmist) has not yet occurred. Perhaps we should recognize this as a 'prophetic' perfect, the confidence of faith in the faithfulness of God to bring to completion a yet unfulfilled future, despite every experience to the contrary, despite all of the unanswered 'why' questions, despite even a persisting sense of present forsakenness. This expression of unqualified completion, in the face of desolation and despair, is the psalmist's last word.

Dear Lord,
your word is replete with promises
yet those promises don't seem as immediate as our circumstances,
nor as immediate and compelling as our feelings.
There are times when we don't feel your presence –
there are many more times when we don't feel that we truly believe.
Help us not to confuse faith with feeling;
help us to trust you despite our feelings and our immediate circumstances;
help us to trust you even in darkness and silence.
For the sake of your Son who endured the darkness and the silence.
Amen.

Chapter Four

Darkness and Israel

For the director of music.
To [the tune of] "The Doe of the Morning."
A psalm of David.

Sadly, the tune 'The Doe of the Morning' is lost to us; we have no
way of knowing its rhythm, its melody, its mood; we have little
assured knowledge of the music of ancient Israel – but that
which we do know, that which is attested in this superscription
(and that which itself is remarkable), is that this very personal
and disarmingly honest psalm was to be set to music, was to be
made available to the worship of Israel.

Whether it is entirely appropriate to designate the psalter as
the hymn book of post-exilic Israel is open to dispute but it is
surely beyond dispute that this collection of songs and poems
was a central resource for Israel's worship, both personal and
corporate and, as such, is significant of the content and form
of Israel's worship, of Israel's perception of God, of Israel's
manner of praise and prayer. Though so little can be known
with certainty of the liturgy of Israel there has been no shortage
of attempts (especially in the late nineteenth and twentieth
centuries) at historical reconstruction. One such attempt, still
influential when I was a student, was the positing of a priestly
king cult in ancient Israel, echoing a similar Canaanite cult or
later Babylonian influences, and evidenced by references within
the psalms to the king as a quasi-divine figure, as 'son' of God,
while assuming particular significance for the Hebrew words

translated 'king' (מלך) and 'righteousness' (צדק) with particular interest in their combination with reference to the mysterious figure who encounters Abram in Genesis 14:18ff.[1] Perhaps psalms which speak of the suffering and vindication of Israel's king reflect an ancient cult where the king, as God's representative and embodiment, enacted the dying and rising of the seasons in an annual Autumnal Festival. Such speculations cannot be entirely dismissed – that precisely is their principal problem – we have insufficient knowledge to refute such reconstructions and, correspondingly, we have insufficient knowledge to establish them. The idea is interesting, perhaps intriguing and potentially illuminating, but it remains no more than an idea, an influential instance of the tendency of historical criticism to attempt to peer behind the text, positing possible pre-texts, cultural forms, 'bare' events, authorial intentions – a tendency, in other words, to distract attention from the text itself, albeit with the worthy intention of illuminating the text by speculative reconstruction.

   That this present psalm is superscribed to David (לדוד) renders it vulnerable to such cultic interpretations and, though most commentators identify it as a psalm of individual lament, some categorize it as a royal psalm.[2] While not necessarily associating the psalm with a priestly-king cult at a New Year festival, Sigmund Mowinckel nonetheless asserts more generally that '. . . the I-psalms look at everything from the point of view of the leading person, the king',[3] and that '[n]aturally the illness of the king would be a matter of concern to the whole country'.[4] At face value this seems a reasonable and modest conclusion but even this depends on the significance we accord to the superscription to David – even if this psalm describes the suffering of a king (or even of David himself) are we to hear the psalm as descriptive of the suffering of a king specifically as the king or rather as the suffering of one who merely happens to be the king, the suffering of a king that could as readily be the suffering of anyone else? Here, as elsewhere, I must confess my prejudice. For reasons elaborated in chapters one and two of this book I have vested interest (as I suspect most readers of this

psalm have interest) in hearing this psalm in a manner that resonates with a general and common experience of suffering and
desolation – this is (at least partly) my motivation in not hearing
this psalm in the first instance in relation to the suffering of
Christ, and this similarly is my motivation for resisting any
marginalizing of the psalm to a supposed priestly-king cult or
even to a manner of suffering and desolation that is specific and
peculiar to a king as the king.[5] Holy Scripture is received and
heard within the Church as a means of grace and we should
resist any interpretation or reconstruction that inhibits such a
hearing and receiving. Inasmuch as historical understanding
can enhance, illuminate, and refine a contemporary hearing
of Scripture as a transformative means of grace such understanding should be pursued with discipline and rigour but the
historical scholar needs to be vigilant lest speculative reconstruction distracts from the text itself and lest such reconstruction
asserts an inappropriate distance between the text and its contemporary hearer, rendering the text impotent and of merely
academic antiquarian interest. The concern of an ecclesial
reading of Scripture is not just with what the text says or signifies but with what the text is doing – or, rather, with what the
Holy Spirit may now be saying and doing through this text.

Of potentially greater helpfulness, therefore, have been form
critical attempts (following Artur Weiser and others)[6] to recon-
struct the possible place of this psalm, as a psalm of individual
lament, within the liturgy of later Israel (usually the post-exilic
community). Particular attention here is given to the abrupt
change of mood at verse 22 and to the possibility that some form
of priestly oracle of reassurance lies behind and explains this
change of mood.[7] No reconstructed ancient cultus is implied
here, rather an individual brings a personal lament using the
words of this psalm liturgically, a priest interposes a word of
blessing, and the suppliant responds with the confession of
praise with which the psalm concludes.

Whether or not one holds a sacramental view of Christian
ministry, any Christian minister inevitably and often is placed
in the position of a priest, mediating God's presence and God's

word to someone who is sick or distressed. No one (no matter how 'high' their theology of priestly ministry) would deny that every man and woman has access through Christ and by the Spirit to the Father, but it would be similarly foolish to fail to recognize that God mediates his presence through his creation, that he uses men and women (not to mention the human words of Holy Scripture, the water of Holy Baptism, and the bread and wine of Holy Communion) to mediate his presence.[8] Those who serve as chaplains in hospitals and hospices (especially) but also in prisons, in military service, or more generally in industry and commerce will be very familiar with the dynamic, with the need and responsibility, not merely to bring a word of comfort or reassurance, but, by the Spirit, to be the means of God's presence and God's grace. The experience of Job's friends should caution us concerning the theologically proper but wholly inappropriate word – they were doing well when they simply 'sat on the ground with him for seven days and seven nights' not saying a word (Job 2:13). The spell-checker on the very first word processing package I used back in the mid 1980s didn't recognize the word 'pastor' and continually wanted to change it to 'pester' – not entirely inappropriate to some more pompous expressions of pastoral ministry that haven't learnt the lesson of Job's friends. The pastoral and priestly calling is to be a means of God's presence above and beyond the conveying of information. Pastors should be more concerned to serve as effective priests than to peddle platitudes or proffer explanations – not least because there are no explanations; here and now suffering remains a mystery to be endured rather than a problem to be resolved.

It is entirely possible, then, to hear this psalm as an invitation to an appropriately pastoral and priestly intervention, to the presence and reassurance that can move the plaintiff from the first part of the psalm to its conclusion, from despair and desolation to renewed trust and hope – it is possible but, as I maintained in the last chapter, it is not a necessary interpretation of the text and it may not be a valid interpretation. If, within the liturgical use of the psalm within the worship of Israel, some priestly oracle was interjected before verse 22, the text itself bears no witness to the fact other than the entirely unexplained change of mood at this verse.[9] The attractiveness of explanations for this change of mood does not of itself constitute evidence in support of such explanations. What we know with absolute certainty – and far more simply – is that this psalm of personal lament, with its devastating expression of abandonment, was made available to the worship of the people of Israel, was set to music, was sung. And, of course, it was not novel; it was not a genre all to itself; the psalter as we have it includes many laments, both corporate and individual, some of which in certain respects are even more devastating than this. Might it not, therefore, be rather more appropriate to speculate concerning the significance of the inclusion of such psalms as this for the form and manner of Israel's worship? Here, surely we may assume, is a liturgy that gives space and form to complaint, to despair, to expressions of forsakenness. Here is a liturgy that gives space and form to expressions that come close to questioning God's integrity and faithfulness. Here are prayers and confessions that are refreshingly honest about human sin and sinfulness, both individual and corporate, but that are similarly ruthlessly honest in questioning God's own covenant consistency. And, while within the psalter these prayers of lament are surrounded by (and outnumbered by) prayers of praise and thanksgiving, the latter do not in anyway detract from the starkness or moderate the starkness of the former. Whatever else the composition of the psalter signifies, it witnesses to an understanding of God as one who honours honesty and hates hype, who values integrity above sacrifice.[10] The man or woman coming to worship the God of Israel with such a resource of songs and poems would have found little difficulty in identifying psalms that honestly reflected personal circumstances and personal feelings, psalms that expressed in words that which perhaps, more personally, was beyond expression. Certainly the worship of Israel encouraged participation in praise and thanksgiving but not to the point of silencing expressions of complaint and despair.[11]

And what was true for post-exilic Israel was true from the beginning for the Christian Church. The Gospels record Jesus singing a 'hymn' – presumably one of the psalms traditionally sung at Passover – with his disciples before going to Gethsemane (Matthew 26:30; Mark 14:26), and Paul and Silas sing 'hymns' (can we assume 'psalms'?) in prison at Philippi (Acts 16:25); the church at Ephesus are encouraged to '[s]peak to one another with psalms, hymns and spiritual songs' (Ephesians 5:19) and the encouragement is repeated to the church at Colossae as an outworking of what it may mean to '[l]et the word of Christ dwell in you richly' (Colossians 3:16). While it may be anachronistic to speak of a 'canon' of the Old Testament Scriptures in use by the earliest Church, all evidence suggests that the psalter, pretty much as we know it, was treasured by the Church from the beginning. And such is hardly surprising: in the first place, from the beginning, the Church had come to hear so many of these psalms, and this psalm in particular, with reference to Christ, but, more generally and simply, the appeal and appropriateness of the psalms to the worship of the Church would have been of the same manner as their appeal within the worship of Second Temple Judaism – here, in these ancient words, are sentiments that resonate with any authentic worshipping community as they come in praise, in prayer, in petition, and also in lament. Understandably, therefore, as the liturgy of the Church in both East and West was developed, the recitation, chanting, or singing of the psalms gave structure and content to the Church's disciplined order of prayer. Today, when I come to read the daily office in any of its forms and versions, I will read, chant, or sing several psalms in the course of a single day. Here today I find words which express my praise and thanksgiving far more profoundly than any words I could muster, and here too, ideally, I should find words that, with a disarming honesty repudiate any pretence of false piety, put into words a sense of despair and forsakenness more starkly than I would dare attempt. The sad qualification to this affirmation and commendation is that more recent lectionaries have been less than comprehensive and, in particular, have been sparing in their inclusion of psalms of lament, a matter compounded for the Church of England by the increasing prominence of Eucharistic worship – a development to be welcomed were it not for the frequent omission of psalms in the implementing of current Anglican Eucharistic liturgies. That this psalm, along with many others, has become precious to me is because it expresses what I would want to say more graphically and candidly than any words that I could form and, more specifically, it has been the means through which I have been enabled to pray at times when I was incapable of bringing words of my own.

Over the centuries, philosophical theology has expended much time, paper, and ink in pondering the 'problem' of suffering and evil. If God is wholly good surely he would will there to be no suffering; if God is wholly powerful surely he would be able to fulfil his own good will; but suffering continues, therefore surely God cannot be both wholly good and wholly powerful. Attempts to justify God in the context of the continuing reality of suffering – arguments known as theodicy – have taken a variety of sometimes conflicting and sometimes complementary forms. Rarely has God's goodness been questioned (by Christian theologians, at least) but the notion has sometimes been qualified by the recognition that God's goodness is higher than our perception of goodness and therefore may include that which we might now perceive as evil but which is ultimately good. Specifically, God is good in the context of human sin and therefore his goodness includes acts of judgement (here, of course, we come close to the arguments of Job's friends which, we should remember, prove no more persuasive to God than to Job). Related to this line of argument (though not identical to it) is the notion of the greater good, usually identified by the Latin phrase *O felix culpa* (Oh happy fault), an argument proposing that the revelation of God's glory is enhanced (and thereby the ultimate happiness of humankind is enhanced) through Adam's sin and its appalling consequences. Alternatively, some arguments have proposed that God's power and freedom is limited by the freedom and integrity of creation and, more specifically, by human freedom. More recently this latter form of argument has taken more radical form in the notion that God is at least partly if not wholly identified with the processes of creation, that God himself is in the process of 'becoming'. The oddity which should impress itself upon the reflective reader is the absence of such arguments (with the unfortunate exception of the speeches of Job's friends) in Holy Scripture. The question 'why' is posed repeatedly throughout Scripture, not least in the Psalms, but, aside from the one series of well-intentioned but futile arguments, no answer is attempted. The only valid response to the question 'why' that we encounter in Scripture is the response of lament – and this remains the only valid response. The appropriate theological response to suffering, our own and that of others, is not theodicy – the attempt to explain suffering and to justify God in the face of suffering – but lament.[12]

Through the resource of the psalter, the traditional liturgy of the Church, following the liturgy of Israel, has been rich with lament and thereby remained pastorally realistic and pertinent. Sadly, one must seriously question whether this remains the case, not just as an outcome of unhelpfully selective lectionaries, but more radically within the evangelical and 'Free' churches with which I am most familiar. The Baptist church in which I spent my youth may have been unusual even in the late 1950s and early 1960s but, along with four hymns, two prayers, an Old Testament and a New Testament reading, and a sermon, the morning service included at least one chanted psalm. Perhaps, earlier in the twentieth century, chanting would not have been so unusual amongst Baptist churches: the *Baptist Church Hymnal*, first published in 1900 and revised in 1933, was accompanied by a companion volume of chants and anthems[13] – I think it unlikely that even a charitable press would publish a volume unless it was expected to be widely used. While such older collections of hymns certainly contained a higher proportion of hymns that were meditative and reflective than most contemporary collections, I can think of no hymn, ancient or modern, that comes close to the bleakness of despair that we encounter in this and so many other psalms, but, all the time a collection of hymns was supplemented by the singing (or even the reading) of psalms, lament maintained a prominent place even in Free church liturgy. The desire to be 'contemporary' and 'relevant', the advent of the charismatic movement, and the effective abdication of direct responsibility for worship by not a few Evangelical ministers has changed beyond recognition the ethos of worship in most Baptist churches and other Free churches of evangelical persuasion. In so many churches the art of leading in extempore prayer, both in praise and intercession, has fallen into disuse. It is now rare, in many Free churches, for there to be more than one reading of Scripture and a psalm generally will only be read if it comprises the passage on which the sermon is based. The liturgy of the 'hymn/prayer sandwich' which, for all its inadequacies, at least gave prominence to prayer and the reading of Scripture, has given way to a liturgy of song-singing to the degree that, in some circles, a 'time of worship' has become synonymous with a time of singing songs. It is ironic to reflect that some early English Baptists entirely repudiated the singing of hymns or songs. No collection of hymns or songs has ever been flawless, and every generation of the Christian Church has managed to produce its fair share of poetic and musical dross, but it is probably not unfair to say that the majority of contemporary songs are up-beat in tempo and that the balance between the affective and the confessional and declaratory (with some notable exceptions) has swung in favour of the former. Occasionally one encounters a contemporary attempt at lament but, in at least one case that comes to mind, the impact is neutralized by a tune that would not be out of place in vaudeville.

As intimated earlier, the inadequacy of this liturgy of song singing is significantly compounded by the abdication by so many Free church ministers of any direct responsibility for worship. A music group is re-designated a 'worship' group, with the ability to play an instrument being the only apparent qualification for the bearing of this responsibility. The leading of worship is a theological task, requiring significant theological reflection, and without that reflection (or the facility for that reflection) worship is reduced to the singing of one song after another, often for no better reason than the personal preferences of the musician leading the worship; there is little sense of direction, progression, or journey. Moreover, the leading of worship is an extraordinarily totalitarian process: I could attempt a crossword puzzle during a sermon (I never have done so, but the temptation has occasionally been overwhelming) but a worship leader tells me to stand or to sit and leaves me little option but to participate in whatever is being sung regardless of my personal circumstances or mental and spiritual disposition. In recent years I have made a pact with myself never to sing anything that I couldn't say with integrity – this has issued in regular embarrassing silences on my part, both in College chapel and in local church services.

I realize that all this has the sound of a rant but it is written with not a little embarrassment and troubled conscience. In one way or another I have been involved in the charismatic movement from its beginnings; for a dozen years I was pastor of a decidedly charismatic Baptist church; with the goal of encouraging the participation of others and the identifying of gifts, I was one who effectively abdicated direct responsibility for the leading of worship – and it remains one of my deepest regrets. Some years ago, in conversation with a dear friend, I likened the first few years of my time at Catford to the digging of my spurs in the side of a horse while in the later years I was pulling on the reins for all I was worth – the former years were markedly more effective than the latter; once this particular 'demon' has escaped from the bottle it is almost impossible to entice it to return; it is easier to delegate responsibility than to retrieve it. In some measure of self-defence, it was never the intention to initiate this front-led tyranny of song singing but rather to facilitate a greater openness to the Holy Spirit and to the active participation of members of the church and congregation – something somewhere went disastrously wrong.

Ironically, that which so many pastors of my generation initiated for the sake (in part) of greater participation and contemporary relevance has issued in a form of worship that generally excludes participation and is mind-numbingly tedious. Little could be more tedious than the repetitive singing of one song after another, not least when the variety of those songs from week to week tends to be so limited. Any sense of movement from praise through confession and thanksgiving, through word and response in intercession and petition, has been abandoned in favour (at best) of the attempt to create an atmosphere. What may initially have all the attraction of the lively and the contemporary, for all but the most prejudiced, quickly degenerates into the dull and predictable. Here at the most basic and superficial level is a reason why so many churches which have adopted this pattern, though they may have an encouragingly big 'front door' have a disturbingly big 'back door'.

But the more serious and presently pertinent failure of this liturgy of song singing is that it is so blatantly excluding. This style of worship focuses almost exclusively on praise, adoration, and thanksgiving, usually at quite up-beat tempo, with clapping and other expressions of unqualified exuberance. Nor is this unremitting cheerfulness mitigated by more thoughtful, reflective, and inclusive prayers – more often than not, interjected prayers sustain the mood of joyfulness and gratitude, sometimes (frankly) in disturbingly superficial manner, offered by a 'worship leader', entirely unprepared, highly repetitive, and liberally interspersed with the vocalized punctuation marks of 'Lord', 'just', 'really', and 'great'. Yes, God is 'truly wonderful' but it would be refreshing and edifying to hear the affirmation elaborated with content and description. The presence of children prompts the very worst from this style of worship with trivializing songs that provide sufficient cause for any thoughtful child, approaching adulthood, to jettison Christianity along with Father Christmas and Fairy Godmothers. I have heard God described as 'big' (when he is beyond comparison) and 'complicated' (when he is uniquely simple), and I am weary of being asked to welcome the Spirit (when the Spirit is already present) and thanking the 'Father' for 'coming to die for us'. Moreover, the totalitarian manner of this form of worship renders it difficult to opt out, to observe, to sit, and to pray quietly while the performance proceeds. For the person who comes as this psalmist comes, for the person wrestling with any form of clinical depression, for the person tortured by the breaking down of relationships, for the recently bereaved, for those who have just been told of terminal illness (their own or that of a loved one), all this is unrelieved torture.

The style of worship that I am criticizing, a style now to be experienced in so many British Baptist churches week by week (though the style is by no means exclusive to the Baptist family) represents, I think, the most extreme form of this liturgical exclusivity. But any liturgy of worship that does not include regular and broad engagement with the psalter could, in these respects, be similarly faulted. I know of no other worship resource that includes such proportion, breadth, and depth, not just of lament, both corporate and individual, but of an extraordinary range of human emotions and responses. Time and again the psalmists put into words, with disarming candour, feelings and prayers that most of us would struggle to express but echo nonetheless. Am I angry with God? – there are psalms that name this anger. Am I isolated and opposed? – there are psalms that express this loneliness. Am I despairing of justice in human society or international relations? – that same despair finds voice here. Am I fearful concerning the future for myself and for those I love? – there are psalms that reassure me that I in not alone in such fears. It should not surprise us that the psalms give voice to this range of emotions – they are the common stuff of human experience and spiritual life in every age – what should surprise us (and trouble us) is that this range and candour finds expression so rarely and so poorly in so many collections of hymns and songs and that it is so seldom expressed in forms of contemporary worship that have abandoned the liturgical discipline of the psalms and canticles of Scripture. If I come to so much that passes as contemporary worship fearful, angry, troubled, or despairing I find nothing that enables my coming before God honestly, truthfully. I am excluded. Perhaps I would be better advised to stay in my room, reading the

Scriptures, and echoing the psalms as my own prayers before God (and sometimes, sadly, this is precisely what I have done). I'm not encouraging anyone to withdraw from corporate worship but what should I do when the alternative is dishonesty? Is the greater error the withdrawing or the excluding from which it issues?

The dilemma, then, is an issue of integrity. Neither is it, I suspect, a merely personal or private issue. On any given Sunday in any congregation (of any denomination) just what proportion come bubbling over with ecstatic cheerfulness and what proportion come anxious, confused, disillusioned? I have no way of telling (though the proportion of psalms of praise and psalms of lament may give a clue). Any liturgy of worship that excludes lament, therefore, is not just carelessly exclusive, it is encouraging dishonesty and unreality – and if the psalms and the Scriptures generally tell me anything they tell me that God looks for honesty rather than pretence; the Scriptures offer me no encouragement whatsoever to take refuge in fantasy. Here, I suspect, is the more profound reason for some apparently lively and flourishing churches having 'big back doors': that which initially was attractive and contemporary proves ultimately superficial and non-sustaining; '[h]ope deferred makes the heart sick' (Proverbs 13:12); the promise of unrelenting exuberance proves hollow; there is nothing here of sufficient weight to sustain faith through oppression and pain; like the seed sown on rocky ground, initial enthusiasm withers in the scorching heat of personal tragedy, opposition, and despair (Matthew 13:1ff.).

Every question of this nature, of course, is a question of underlying theology as much as of presenting (and consequent) practice. I would be surprised if there were not some reading this who would vigorously defend the dominance of praise in contemporary worship and repudiate entirely what they would view as a self-indulgent wallowing in negativity that was a denial of the gospel. Surely the Church is not in the same place as was Israel, especially in terms of promise and fulfilment? Surely the move from the Old to the New Testament is a move that takes us beyond lament and turns sorrow to joy? Surely the desolation of the Cross is overwhelmed by resurrection triumph? Surely, in the presence of the God of the gospel 'our problems disappear'[114]? What triumphalistic (and highly damaging) nonsense!

In the first place, I am not arguing for an unremitting and unrelieved diet of lament: there are more psalms of praise, of adoration, of declaration, than there are psalms of lament – I am merely arguing that our worship should not be shaped exclusively by the former without representative inclusion of the latter. Of course I believe that the resurrection overwhelms the Cross, but not in a way that negates it or obscures it: it is the crucified one who is risen just as it is the risen one who was crucified; the risen and ascended Christ still bears the marks of slaughter. The Old Testament is to the New Testament as is shadow to fulfilment, but God hasn't changed and neither has human nature or human experience; this creation is still not as God would ultimately have it to be; creation and we within it are still 'groaning as in the pains of childbirth' (Romans 8:22); we are not yet what fully we shall be. My purpose is not to encourage a self-indulgent wallowing in negativity but rather to make space for realism and honesty – to make precisely that space for integrity that is reflected in the psalter.

The triumphalistic theology that, I suspect, underlies certain contemporary approaches to worship is unprecedentedly damaging – as noted earlier, for the overwhelming majority of the Church's history its liturgy, through sustained inclusion of the psalter, gave voice to the range of honest human responses and emotions. The exclusion of such human honesty through a monochrome (and monotonous) liturgy of song singing and the repression and denial of that honesty through an underlying triumphalism is damaging for all the reasons previously stated, implying the spiritual failure of those who would come before God honestly owning their despair and pain. But even more seriously, this triumphalistic theology is fundamentally erroneous; contrary to its assumptions, it is a denial of the gospel. The appeal of this chapter to those who seek to be shaped biblically in their worship, discipleship, and ecclesial life is to be more thoroughly and comprehensively biblical, to reflect the proportionality of the Scriptures in general and of the psalms in particular. Perhaps Paul's second letter to the Corinthians should be recognized as a sustained repudiation of a triumphalistic misconstruing of the gospel:[15] the apostle rejoices in the one 'who always leads us in triumphal procession in Christ' (2 Corinthians 2:14) but he does so as one who knew 'the sufferings of Christ flow over' into his life (1:5), who 'despaired even of life' (1:8), who carried this treasure in a jar of clay (4:7), who carried around the death of Jesus in his body (4:10) – perhaps Paul's refusal to 'lose heart' (4:16), even in such pressured circumstances, parallels the surprising confession that concludes Psalm 22. There is no resurrection without the Cross; there is no Christian discipleship other than under its shadow; there is no Christian ministry without participating in the sufferings of Christ. Famously, in the Heidelberg Disputation of 1518 (and elsewhere), Martin Luther repudiated a theology of glory (*theologia gloria*) in favour of a theology of the cross (*theologia crucis*):[16] those who seek a theology of glory are seeking God in other place and form than that in which supremely he has revealed himself. The Cross of Christ stands at the heart of the Christian gospel and at the heart of Christian discipleship – and specifically to that Cross. And to the cry of Jesus from that Cross, a cry that at least echoes this psalm, we now turn.

Dear Lord,
  in a world characterized by so much pretence
  it is such relief to pray to one who honours honesty.
  You know our hearts, in any case;
  you know the pain we carry, the fears that oppress, the despair
  that engulfs;
  you know the disillusionment that would mask your light
  and leave us in darkness.
  Forgive us, dear Lord, for every attempt to hide from you.
  Thank you that you are more than sufficient to handle our fears,
  our anger, our desolation.

Without shame we turn to you again
in the name of Jesus, the one who cried out in honest
forsakenness,
Amen.

Chapter Five

Christ's Human Darkness

At the sixth hour darkness came over the whole land until the ninth hour.

And at the ninth hour Jesus cried out in a loud voice, *"Eloi, Eloi, lama sabachthani?"*—which means, "My God, my God, why have you forsaken me?"

When some of those standing near heard this, they said, "Listen, he's calling Elijah."

Someone ran, filled a sponge with wine vinegar, put it on a stick, and offered it to Jesus to drink. "Now leave him alone. Let's see if Elijah comes to take him down," he said.

With a loud cry, Jesus breathed his last.

The curtain of the temple was torn in two from top to bottom. And when the centurion, who stood there in front of Jesus, heard his cry and[1] saw how he died, he said, "Surely this man was the Son[2] of God!"

(Mark 15:33–39)

If the Gospel narratives are recognized as the focal point of the Christian Scriptures, and the passion narratives are recognized as the focal point of the Gospels, then probably Christ's cry of dereliction is rightly perceived as the focal point of Christ's passion – at least as that passion is recorded in the Gospels of Matthew and Mark. In the light of all that has preceded in these Gospel accounts, this cry of God-forsakenness on the lips of Jesus shocks us and intimates something of the genuine depth of horror that was his crucifixion. That the beloved Son, the one with whom the Father is 'well pleased' (Mark 1:11), the one who is the proclaimer and bearer of the kingdom, should now be forsaken and abandoned by his Father to a torturous death in isolation and darkness is simply not what we would have expected on the basis of the preceding narrative. Something inside us protests against this apparent reversal, this seemingly incomparable injustice, this futility and contradiction. It is, then, hardly surprising that we feel the desire to mitigate the desolation and, throughout Christian history, various attempts have been made to qualify what otherwise might be perceived as a bleaker and far more treacherous betrayal than that of Judas. But the narrative of the Gospels will not allow us to evade this desolation or to minimize it, and a significant proportion of this present chapter will be devoted to the repudiation of three ways by which this horror might be lessened.

In the first place, and in counterpoint to much of the argument at the beginning of chapter three of this book, we should resist any attempt to mitigate the desolation of Jesus' cry by assuming it to be a conscious and deliberate citation of the first verse of the twenty-second psalm. That the Church, from its beginning, associated this cry of dereliction with the psalm and, consequently, came to interpret the psalm in the light of Christ's crucifixion is both understandable and appropriate – the mocking of the crowd, the dividing of garments and casting of lots, not to mention the Septuagint's reference to the piercing of hands and feet, all resonate with the details of the passion narratives. But just as we ought not to allow this appropriate and understandable association to deflect us from hearing the psalm also and primarily as the recounting of a more general and common suffering and desolation, so too we ought not to allow this association in any way to lessen the despair and the shock of Jesus' cry. Much of my personal interaction with the psalm, as I have previously explained, derives from the possibility of using this, together with other similar prayers of Scripture, to express my own sense of despair when I cannot muster words of my own that seem sufficient. Jesus certainly would have known

the psalm, would often have heard it read in Hebrew in the syn-
agogue, may well have been able to recite it himself – this
familiarity may well have prompted his cry, but this is not to
reduce the cry to mere recitation; we must not allow this association in our minds and perhaps in the mind of Jesus to detract at
all from the genuineness, the immediacy, and the integrity of his
own utter despair. The psalm puts into words the despair of
forsakenness, not merely the despair of dire and threatening circumstances, but the more profound and disturbing despair of
feeling abandoned by God to those circumstances. That our
sense of despair echoes the despair of the psalmist detracts not
one wit from the reality and singularity of our despair nor does
it detract from the psalmist's despair. That Jesus' cry of dereliction echoes the despair of the psalmist doesn't lessen or qualify
the reality and singularity of his despair, of his sense of abandonment by God, of his unique pathos. What is expressed on
the Cross is Christ's own desolation, not the mere reiteration of
the desolation of another.

In this respect we should note the confusion regarding the
language in which Jesus utters this cry: we would expect some
degree of confusion when a Semitic language is transliterated
into Greek – this may explain the differences between the cry as
recorded in Matthew's Gospel and in Mark's Gospel; alternatively, it may be that one records the cry in Hebrew and the other
in Aramaic (though we really cannot be certain),[3] but can this
confusion of language explain the rather odd assumption of the
crowd that Jesus was calling for Elijah (we would expect them
to have recognized a direct quotation)? This strange response
on the part of the crowd could be a deliberate and mocking
perversity or it could even be the Gospel writers themselves
making a link with the theme of Elijah and his expected coming
as mentioned earlier in the Gospels.[4] Possibly, however, there
are even textual reasons for not hearing this cry as a simple and
direct quotation of the psalm; possibly, even allowing for the
uncertainties of transliteration, the cry of Jesus is simply not a
direct quotation; possibly, then, there are linguistic bases that
would reinforce the theological imperative of hearing this cry

immediately, directly, and unequivocally as the expression of Jesus' own sense of forsakenness.

A common motivation for hearing Jesus' cry as a conscious citation of the psalm is the possibility of his citing the first verse of the psalm with the whole of the psalm, including its concluding hopeful confession, in mind. For Jesus to cry out in apparent God-forsakenness but nonetheless mindful of the concluding and positive confession of the psalm obviously qualifies the despair of his cry, opens the possibility of a conscious expectation of resurrection and vindication, and accords with the more conquering and calm accounts of the passion that we find in Luke and John.[5] It is not at all surprising that several commentators and theologians have fastened on this possibility for persuasive theological reasons – but hardly for persuasive textual reasons: neither in Matthew's Gospel nor in Mark's is there any other word on the lips of the crucified Jesus that would be suggestive of such hopefulness, indeed, in the narratives of the crucifixion in Matthew and Mark these words of abandonment are the only intelligible words that Jesus utters on the Cross; in both Gospels the Temple curtain is rent, in both Gospels the overseeing centurion makes a surprising confession, but these positive hints hardly justify the assumption that this cry of despair is mitigated by a conscious remembering of a positive conclusion; moreover, Mark compounds the bleakness by the abrupt ending of the earliest manuscripts of the Gospel, with the announcement 'He has risen' but with no appearance of the resurrected Jesus and with the women who hear this message too afraid to tell of it – some assume that an original extended ending has been lost but it is not impossible that this abrupt ending is intended, that Mark is using literary means to leave his narrative open, uncertain, and thereby disturbing and provoking.[6] Tempting though it might be to mitigate Jesus' cry of forsakenness with the more hopeful conclusion of the psalm there is no textual reason for doing so, indeed, there is textual (not to mention theological) reason for not hearing this cry at all as a conscious quotation of the psalm.[7]

The next and perhaps more common way of mitigating this cry of forsakenness is by a premature combining and harmonizing of disarmingly distinct Gospel narratives. So accustomed are we, in both the Catholic and Protestant traditions, to meditations and sermons on the words of Jesus from the Cross that I suspect many Christians, without referring to the text, would not be able to distinguish the accounts or to apportion the sayings and incidents to the Gospels in which they occur. On even cursory examination, we have three very different (and surely independent?) accounts of the passion with even Matthew and Mark, for all their similarities, differing in significant detail.[8] Matthew, Mark, and Luke suggest the 'Last Supper' to be a Passover celebration with Jesus being executed the following day; John has Jesus being crucified as the Passover lambs are being slaughtered – Joachim Jeremias suggests a coherent way of reconciling this distinction historically, but it is equally possible that John, who apart from possible interpretations of the 'Bread of Life' discourse (John 6:25ff.) offers no account of the institution of the Lord's Supper, is making a theological point by narrative means.[9] Matthew, Mark, and Luke record a darkness over the land from the sixth until the ninth hour, while Mark adds the detail that Jesus was crucified at the third hour, but John has Jesus still before Pilate at the sixth hour and makes no mention of the darkness. All four Gospels have the soldiers dividing Jesus' clothes but only John gives detail of this and, in the earliest manuscripts at least, only John draws attention to the anticipation of this in Psalm 22. Matthew and Mark have Jesus offered wine mixed with gall (Matthew) or myrrh (Mark) when he is first crucified and which he refuses. All four Gospels have Jesus later offered wine vinegar – in the case of Matthew and Mark this follows the cry of dereliction; in Luke it is part of the soldiers' mockery; in John it follows Jesus' request 'I am thirsty'. Only Matthew and Mark include the cry of dereliction. Matthew, Mark, and Luke record the tearing of the Temple curtain, but only Matthew records an earthquake and the 'raising to life' of many 'holy people'. In Mark's account, the centurion declares 'Surely this man was the Son of God' (though even here the confession could be interpreted more hesitantly);[10] in Matthew, notwithstanding the optimist translation suggested by the *NIV*, the words again may be more hesitant 'Surely he was [a] son of God';[11] Luke's centurion is more hesitant still (or, at least, less explicitly 'Christological'), 'Surely this was a righteous man';[12] John makes no mention of the centurion.

In Luke and in John, Jesus has rather more to say than in Matthew and Mark – though to notice merely this is probably to miss the point. In Luke and John, Jesus is rather less the victim than in Matthew and Mark; rather more in control than the apparent control of the priests, the mob, Pilate, and the soldiers. In Luke's narrative, Jesus, on the way to the Cross, urges the 'Daughters of Jerusalem' to weep not for him but for themselves. It is in this Gospel alone that Jesus, as he is being crucified, prays 'Father, forgive them…' (though these words are omitted in some manuscripts). Similarly it is here alone that Jesus promises 'paradise' to one of the criminals crucified alongside him. And in Luke's Gospel, Jesus breathes his last with the confident prayer 'Father, into your hands I commit my spirit'. It is in John's Gospel that we find an extended account of Jesus' trial before Pilate, an account where Jesus attests that Pilate would have no power over him unless it had been given from above. It is here that Jesus addresses his mother from the Cross together with the mysterious 'disciple whom he loved'. It is here alone (as we have already noted) that Jesus says 'I am thirsty', and, in John's Gospel, Jesus 'gives up his spirit' with the possibly triumphant cry 'It is finished' ($\tau\epsilon\tau\epsilon\lambda\epsilon\sigma\tau\alpha\iota$). Perhaps most notably, however, in contrast to Jesus' cry of abandonment in Matthew and Mark, John concludes his very different and extended account of the 'upper room' discourse with Jesus affirming that, even though his disciples forsake him, he is not alone but the Father is with him. There immediately follows the 'High Priestly' prayer of John 17 in which Jesus, as previously, speaks of his Cross as his 'glory'.

How, then, should we respond to these extraordinary differences, to the contrast between Jesus assured of his Father's constant presence and Jesus crying out in abandonment; between one who otherwise remains silent and one who speaks words of comfort and forgiveness; between one who finally cries out in a loud voice and one who confidently commits himself to his Father, one who affirms that 'it is finished'? The temptation, of course, is to try to harmonize these different narratives, to work them together and to smooth away their distinctions. Countless well-intentioned nineteenth-century lives of Christ, together with more sophisticated harmonies of the Gospels and even the *Diatessaron* of the Early Church issue from this understandable but (I think) misguided motivation. With not dissimilar effect but perhaps distinct intention, historical criticism attempts to penetrate behind these narratives to the bare event of Golgotha, to a dispassionate approximation to what really happened or, perhaps more helpfully, to a tentative reconstruction of the distinct communities to which these narratives were originally addressed. But might there not be reasons for disowning all these speculative reconstructions as not merely futile but inappropriate, misconceived, and even possibly faithless? Christian faith, of course, rests on the confidence that Jesus actually was crucified in our human history but we have no given and authoritative access to that historical event other than the distinct and very different witnesses that are these Gospels – it is these Gospels, rather than attempted reconstructions of what may lie behind them, that are heard and received by the Church as means of grace, as canonical, as authoritative. Moreover, the Gospel writers, though certainly not unconcerned to relate historical fact,[13] seem to be concerned not merely with historical fact but appear similarly concerned to interpret that historical fact, to witness to that historical fact, to elicit response. Their distinct accounts are unapologetically witness, unapologetically interpretative, unapologetically theological. A faithful and open response to these distinct witnesses is to hear their testimonies in all their distinctiveness, to permit these authors to be heard with their own voice without muffling that voice with premature attempts to harmonize and unify.

Luke and John, albeit in rather different manner, bear witness to the crucified Jesus as no mere victim, for all the agonies of the

Cross. They portray the crucified one as nonetheless the Son of the Father, and even at the Cross they peer through the Cross to forgiveness and reconciliation, to completion, to glory. Matthew and Mark, no less than Luke and John, proclaim the crucified one as the Son of the Father, as risen, as undefeated – but they do so by rather different means and they do so in a manner that enables us to hear the full horror of the desolation which was the Cross. We hear these different testimonies as complementary, but not complementing one another in any way that dulls or qualifies the distinctive witness of each. We hear the compassion and confidence of Luke and John without allowing their witnesses to soften the horror of desolation in Matthew and Mark. We hear the desolation of Matthew and Mark without lessening the more confident testimony of Luke and John. Each Gospel writer brings a distinct and faithful perspective on the Cross which we must hear in its full and unmuffled force: it is the case that Jesus is crucified, as the Son confident in the Father, mindful of those who love him, those who acknowledge him, and those who despise him, mock him, and kill him; but it is also the case that Jesus is crucified as one who is truly human and, as truly human, bears the agony and protests the abandonment that are in no sense lessened by that intimate obedience to the Father that brought him to this place of horror.

Which brings us to a third and probably most common means of mitigating the cry of dereliction recorded in Matthew and Mark. Jesus is truly human but he is also truly and fully God – and God (the Church traditionally has affirmed) is beyond suffering. This assumed and confessed divine impassibility led all to easily in the Early Church to the mirror imaged denials that are docetism (God does not suffer therefore Jesus only seemed to be truly human and only seemed to suffer) and adoptionism (God does not suffer therefore Jesus, as one who is truly human and truly suffers, cannot be truly God). There are some breathtaking assumptions about God here, about who God is, about what God can or cannot do – and we will explore these assumptions in chapter seven of this book. Our concern at this point is merely to admit how easily, then and now, an appropriate confession of Jesus' divinity can slip into an effective denial of his humanity and of the reality of his suffering. As a child I was horrified by the thought of Christ's Cross and now, with some embarrassment, admit that, in childlike but heretical naïveté, I assumed that it would somehow have been different for him; that, being God, he could effectively rise above it – but I can't help wondering how many adult Christians, in sentimental piety, continue to entertain my childish assumptions. Perhaps I should mention that, within the theological context in which I grew up, the cry of dereliction was viewed not primarily as an expression of a mere human sense of abandonment but rather as an outcome of a quite specific divine drama of sin-bearing, a unique and therefore unparalleled abandonment – I will postpone a discussion of this latter assumption until the next chapter.

Albeit with limited success, the Early Church tried to resolve these questions of Christ's true deity and true humanity at the Council of Chalcedon in 451. Positively, those gathered there simply affirmed that Jesus, who is of one and the same essence as the Father in his deity, is also of one and same essence as us in his humanity,[14] like us in every way apart from sin.[15] Negatively, the council affirmed that these two natures concurred in the single person (or subsistence) of Christ 'without confusion, without change, without division, without separation'.[16] I once heard Robert Jenson describe the council as a typical ecumenical attempt at accommodation, a defining of the boundaries of orthodox faith by isolating that which must be denied rather than an attempt to penetrate that which should be affirmed. Even in this limited goal the council was less than fully successful: at best its affirmations came to be interpreted and developed rather differently in the Western Church than in the Eastern Church; at worst it never gained the assent of many Eastern churches and believers. It is one thing to affirm that the single person of Christ is at the same time both truly and fully human and truly and fully divine, but it is another matter entirely to ponder how this single person can be truly and fully the one without prejudice to being truly and fully the other; how he really can share these two natures both without confusion and without separation, without change and without division. Even amongst the churches of East and West who have accepted the council's definition as the measure of Christological orthodoxy, there are those who have been accused either of Nestorianism (of separating the two natures) or of Eutychianism (of confusing the two natures by assuming that the human is overwhelmed by the divine).

While it is relatively easy (and cheap) to criticize, a moment's honest reflection reveals just how hard it is to affirm Christ's true humanity without prejudice to his true deity and vice versa: this is an exceedingly tricky tight-rope on which to balance. What do we mean by 'nature' in any case and how (other than in abstraction) is nature to be defined? I will return to this question in chapter seven of this book, specifically to the question of what is meant by divine nature and how this might properly be defined in the light of the gospel story. To some degree, chapter six of this book similarly will explore further what is meant by human nature and how this too might properly be defined in the light of the gospel story – for now I simply want to register how easily an affirmation of Christ's true humanity becomes qualified by an affirmation of his true deity in a manner that correspondingly qualifies our hearing of this cry of abandonment and mitigates the agony of the Cross. Whatever we might want to say quite appropriately concerning the Cross, and even this cry of abandonment, as revealing the nature of the one who truly is God, we must do so without prejudice to the truly human suffering that the gospels narrate – indeed I will argue in chapter seven that we will fall short of understanding the Cross as a revelation of God's true nature until we have thoroughly grasped its significance as a revelation of human nature and as a true and unqualified event of human suffering.

It is entirely appropriate that Christian theologians, especially in the last fifty years, have focused attention on this cry of dereliction for our understanding of God (even if that focus has tended to challenge the way in which the Church traditionally has expressed an understanding of God's nature) – as already intimated, I will discuss these developments in chapter seven. Of course this cry of dereliction has immense significance for our understanding of God, for our understanding of the relationship between the Father and the Son by the Spirit, but to raise such questions too quickly is perhaps to overlook the actual language of Christ's protest: he does not cry 'my Father, why have you forsaken me', he cries 'my God, why have you forsaken me', and surely we should be startled, particularly at this juncture, at this surprising change of address. While in Mark's Gospel references to Jesus addressing God as 'Father' are more sparse than in the other Gospels, the narrative begins with Jesus' baptism and with a voice from heaven attesting Jesus as 'my Son' (Mark 1:11). Matthew's narrative, which also includes this cry of dereliction, is far more liberally sprinkled with instances of Jesus addressing God as 'Father' but, most poignantly, both Matthew and Mark record Jesus appealing to God as 'Father' in Gethsemane – here perhaps is the most intimate and poignant moment in the Gospels; here Jesus wrestles with the prospect of the Cross in an agony that rightly is perceived as anticipating this cry of dereliction; yet this 'Father-Son' language of intimate relationship gives way at Golgotha to the seemingly more detached address to 'my God'. Chalcedon cautions us against ever separating or dividing the deity and humanity of Christ; all that Jesus does and is he does and is as one who is truly God and truly human; the one who is son of Mary is also and simultaneously the Son of the Father – but this surprising change of address surely ought to alert us to something truly human occurring here as well as something truly divine, something between a man and God at least as much as something between the Son and the Father. Certainly the agony of Gethsemane should be recognized as interpreting the agony of the Cross – but not to the degree that it distracts us from the significance of the very human form of this agony.

Certainly the suffering of Jesus, as the one who is truly and fully God, is significant and perhaps definitive for an authentically Christian understanding of the nature of God, an understanding of what the word 'God' actually means. Certainly the suffering of Jesus, as the one who is the Son of the Father, is significant and perhaps definitive for an understanding of the immanent Trinitarian relationships between Father, Son, and Holy Spirit. Certainly the suffering of Jesus, as the one who uniquely is truly human, is significant and perhaps definitive for an authentically Christian understanding of human nature, of the sinfulness and fallenness of the human condition, of the relatedness and distinction between God and humanity. But the suffering of Jesus, as one who is truly human, is firstly and most simply significant as authentically human suffering. Appropriately, there are so many theological conclusions to be drawn from this cry and from this suffering, but let them not be drawn in a manner that distracts us from the truly human suffering that occurs here or in any way that mitigates or qualifies that suffering as truly human.

Psalm 22 speaks of a genuinely human suffering, of human rejection, of abuse, of isolation, of humiliation, of a human sense of being abandoned by God – and, whether or not Jesus, in his cry of abandonment, was consciously echoing this psalm, his suffering is paralleled and anticipated here; his suffering, though uniquely his, is authentically human and, in this respect, accessible to us and shared with us. Two criminals were crucified with Jesus and the narrative of John's Gospel suggests that they took longer to die – crucifixion was a common form of execution in the Roman Empire and John's Gospel again suggests that Jesus' suffering on the Cross was unusually and surprisingly brief – throughout human history countless men and women have suffered lingering and torturous deaths and, though perhaps more brief than some, the death of Jesus was lingering and torturous nonetheless. Jesus, like so many others before and since, was spat upon, insulted, mocked, and abused; he suffered and died to the sounds of a jeering mob. Jesus, like so many others, was falsely accused and unjustly condemned, he was subjected to the mockery of a trial before a judge more concerned for the security of his political position than for justice. Jesus, like so many, was abandoned by his friends at the moment of his deepest need; he was left to suffer abuse and torture alone and friendless. Jesus, like others, was betrayed by one close to him, was handed over for a handful of silver coins – and Jesus, unlike most who have been so betrayed, knew that he was being betrayed, offered bread and wine to his betrayer, knelt before his betrayer and washed his feet. Jesus, perhaps like some, knew something of the horrors that were awaiting him and humanly shrank from those horrors with sweat falling like drops of blood to the ground. And Jesus, like so many in the hour of anguish, felt abandoned by God, heard nothing in reply to his cries except the crushing darkness of unremitting silence. And like us all, Jesus died; his cries came to silence; there was no more pain; there was no more consciousness; there was no more anything; like us he was left in a grave to rot, the food for maggots. Jesus' suffering is unique but, before and besides its uniqueness, it is commonplace; it is human suffering; it is our suffering.

In the following two chapters I will attempt to say something about sin and atonement, about the sense in which the suffering of Christ is particular, unique, and definitive, and something about the nature of God as ultimately defined in this event of human suffering, perhaps even something about the questions of theodicy, about the theological and philosophical problems of suffering itself – but none of these issues is the reason motivating the writing of this book; all these are proper theological and philosophical concerns, but they are not the intensely personal concern which motivates this writing.

The Letter to the Hebrews describes Christ as one who is able 'to sympathize with our weaknesses', one 'who has been tempted in every way, just as we are—yet was without sin' (Hebrews 4:15). Sympathy, for some, has degenerated to an offensive and insulting notion, a patronizing sentiment to be rejected. Empathy has become the more acceptable term, the ability to feel the pain of another, to enter into their experience and suffering. Frankly, I find myself puzzled by this rejection and preference: surely it is the claim to feel the pain of another, the claim to be able to enter into their experience and suffering, that is truly patronizing and offensive? My suffering is uniquely mine; others may suffer the same condition but they do so as in their own quite different contexts and as the unique persons that they are. You feel your pain, you recognize my pain, but you can't enter into my pain and it is delusory to pretend otherwise. We should beware of defining words by their root meanings, but the word 'sympathy', at root, means to suffer together with another, not to enter into another's sufferings but to suffer alongside another. In the next chapter I will be arguing that, uniquely, Christ does enter into our suffering and make it his own, he alone can do this and has done it – but the author of the Letter to the Hebrews is making a more common and simply human point: whatever we must say concerning the uniqueness of Christ's suffering and its unique effects, firstly and more simply it is in the continuity of human suffering; he suffers as we suffer; he suffers alongside us; he, therefore, can 'sympathize' with our suffering.

Suffering of any kind is isolating: you feel alone; you are tempted to feel that no one really understands; that no one has suffered in a similar way. Reading the psalms, reading Job, reading Jeremiah – not to mention a host of the more candid Christian biographies – you come to realize that you are not alone; others have known similar pain, similar darkness, similar isolation and abandonment. And coming to read the narratives of Christ's crucifixion, hearing his cry of abandonment, and realizing that this is genuinely human suffering and not some hermetically sealed divine charade, you come to the insight of the Letter to the Hebrews that he too truly suffered, that he understands. When I feel rejection, I know that he also felt rejection. When the darkness oppresses and suffocates, I know that he has been there. When every prayer reverberates in silence, I know that his words too were met with silence. When I feel forsaken by God, abandoned to my circumstances, I hear his cry of desolation. I long for one who really will enter into my pain and rescue me – but company and sympathy will do for 'starters'.

Dear Lord,
once in human history your Son was made human:
he was born as we are born;
he grew as we grow;
he passed through puberty as we pass through puberty;
he knew the love of friends and family as we know human love.
But, once in human history, he was betrayed, falsely accused, and
falsely condemned;
he was deserted by those he loved;
he was abused and humiliated;
he cried out in silence and darkness;
he too felt God-forsaken;
he too died and was buried.
We know that this wasn't the end of his story –
help us, in his name, to know that neither is such desolation the
end of our story.
Amen.

Chapter Six

Christ's Unique Darkness

From the sixth hour until the ninth hour darkness came over all the land.

About the ninth hour Jesus cried out in a loud voice, *"Eloi, Eloi,*[1] *lama sabachthani?"*—which means, "My God, my God, why have you forsaken me?"

When some of those standing there heard this, they said, "He's calling Elijah."

Immediately one of them ran and got a sponge. He filled it with wine vinegar, put it on a stick, and offered it to Jesus to drink. The rest said, "Now leave him alone. Let's see if Elijah comes to save him."

And when Jesus had cried out again in a loud voice, he gave up his spirit.

At that moment the curtain of the temple was torn in two from top to bottom. The earth shook and the rocks split. The tombs broke open and the bodies of many holy people who had died were raised to life. They came out of the tombs, and after Jesus' resurrection they went into the holy city and appeared to many people.

When the centurion and those with him who were guarding Jesus saw the earthquake and all that had happened, they were terrified, and exclaimed, "Surely he was the Son[2] of God!" (Matthew 27:45–54).

All human suffering is unique and particular: though others may suffer the same illnesses, the same pain, the same abuse, the same rejection, they suffer uniquely as the unique people that they are. But all human suffering is human: notwithstanding its particularity and uniqueness, there is an underlying commonality and continuity. The suffering of Christ, like all human suffering, was particular and unique, but it was the concern of the last chapter to argue, nonetheless, that his suffering was truly human suffering, common and continuous with all human suffering. Yet, Christ's suffering was uniquely and particularly his and the precise nature of that particularity, I suspect, has issued in a further basis for removing his suffering from the continuity of our suffering, his cry of abandonment from our apparently similar cries. Part of the horror of so much human suffering is its apparent meaninglessness, its random pointlessness. Certainly virtues of fortitude, patience, hopefulness can be developed and matured through the experience of suffering – but generally in those who are virtuous in the first place and such secondary outcomes hardly justify suffering or render the meaningless meaningful. But Christ's suffering was purposeful with quite specific meaning and outcome, '. . . the Son of Man did not come to be served, but to serve, and to give his life as a ransom for many' (Matthew 20:28; cf. Mark 10:45), and the recognition of this purposefulness tends to specify our hearing of his cry of abandonment and to render it again remote.

I suspect that it is almost impossible for contemporary Western Christians, or indeed any Western Christians since the Reformation, both Catholic and Protestant, to hear Christ's cry of dereliction other than as a quite specific and unique event of forsakenness: on the Cross the sinless Son of God is made sin for us (2 Corinthians 5:21); he bears the penalty which justly is ours; he, as the infinite Son, bears an infinite punishment, an eternity of hell in our place; his sense of forsakenness by the Father is indicative precisely of this penal separation; rather than the crown of thorns, the nails, and the spear, this rupture in the eternal Trinity was the true and unique depth and reality of Christ's suffering on the Cross. His cry of abandonment, therefore, though apparently so similar to a common human sense of abandonment, is of a wholly other order; only in the anguish

of hell is his cry echoed and even there only in a far less profound and less comprehensive sense.[3]

The first cause for pause in this all too familiar interpretation
should be its apparent absence from the crucifixion narratives
in these Gospels. Indeed, apart from the previously mentioned
enigmatic reference to his life as a 'ransom' in Matthew and
Mark, there is no explicit attempt in Matthew, Mark, or Luke, to
offer any explanation or interpretation for Jesus' crucifixion
whatsoever – and this despite repeated affirmations of its inevitability and prophetic necessity. Repentance and forgiveness
are to be proclaimed in his name but the first three gospels offer
no explicit explanation of how this message of forgiveness
relates to the drama of the Cross. John's Gospel, as noted in
the previous chapter, consistently conflates Jesus' crucifixion
with his glory as the means through which he will draw men
and women to himself (John 12:32), identifies his Cross as the
moment of this world's judgement (John 12:31),[4] and (also as
noted previously) records Jesus as being crucified as the Passover lambs are being slaughtered in the Temple – indeed, at the
beginning of John's narrative, Jesus is identified as the Lamb of
God, who takes away the sin of the world' (John 1:29),[5] and the
'Bread of Life' discourse in John 6 (explicitly set in the context of
Passover) further reinforces this underlying theme. In the light
of this Passover focus in John, maybe we should recognize the
'Last Supper' narratives in Matthew, Mark, and Luke as similarly identifying Jesus as the true Passover lamb, as the one
whose body and blood are for us, as the one whose flesh and
blood become truly our food and drink. By sharing in bread and
wine, we now come to participate in the events and benefits of
Christ's passion just as Israel, by sharing in the Passover meal,
come to participate in the events and benefits of the exodus from
Egypt.[6] Significantly too, Paul in the first letter to the Corinthians makes repeated use of Passover imagery and assumes our
participation in bread and wine to signify a participation in
Christ's body and blood (1 Corinthians 5:7f.; 10:14–22).

But this paschal identification falls short of an explanation: it
interprets Christ's sacrifice in continuity with this particular

sacrificial ritual of Israel; it identifies a means through which we come to participate in Christ's sacrifice and its benefits; but it does not at all explain the dynamic of Christ's sacrifice, of why and how this suffering issues in the taking away of sin. And to further compound the problem, in the worship of Israel the Passover sacrifice, a form of redemption (or ransom) offering, was specifically not a sin offering – the Passover meal was to be shared by every member of every family whereas those on behalf of whom a sin offering was made were explicitly excluded from participating in it. The original Passover sacrifice is recorded as being the means through which the first born of Israel are redeemed, the means through which Israel is preserved from judgement and death – but the judgement here is primarily a judgement on Egypt rather than on Israel. And neither here nor in any of the sacrificial rituals of Israel (other than perhaps in the case of the 'scapegoat' – which, as unclean, is specifically not a sacrifice) is there any thought of the sacrificial offering bearing the judgement or punishment of the one who makes the offering: what perhaps is remarkable in the sacrificial rituals of Israel is that neither in Leviticus nor anywhere else are we ever presented with anything remotely resembling an explanation of why and how these rituals are effective; the sacrificial rituals of Israel are simply a provisional means through which Israel's God graciously and at great cost to himself holds his people in covenant relationship despite their sin (the blood, representing the life of the offering, belonged to God rather than to the one bringing the offering).

So what are we to understand by this reference to Jesus as 'the Lamb' who 'takes away sin'?[7] John's Gospel offers no direct explanation, though the imagery of judgement and life, of sin and cleansing, recurs throughout the narrative. When Jesus speaks of 'those who hear' his word and who 'believe him who sent' him not being 'condemned' but having already 'crossed over from death to life' (John 5:24) is it over tenuous to hear this again as a reflection of Passover imagery – though perhaps we should also note here that the term 'condemnation' is a somewhat weighted translation of a word more simply and commonly

translated 'judgement' (κρίσις)? Rather too readily we understand judgement as condemnation and punishment as penalty
whereas (assuming an Old Testament background for the significance of New Testament words and concepts) judgement
should more properly be understood as God acting decisively
to establish righteousness and peace, to put things right, while
punishment is perhaps more properly understood as chastening, a correction that issues in change, purging, cleansing – just
as, within the Old Testament, the imagery of fire and water
overwhelmingly signifies purging rather than destruction. The
Old Testament text that perhaps most commonly has been
heard by the Church in the light of Christ speaks of one who
bore 'the punishment that brought us peace' (Isaiah 53:5) – the
King James Version rather more appropriately translated the
Hebrew word מוסר (musar) as 'chastisement' – not an arbitrary
penalty but a purging corrective. Remarkably, given the contemporary prominence of penal understandings of the
atonement, this is the only text in Holy Scripture that explicitly
links a notion of punishment to Christ's Cross – and, as already
noted, the notion of punishment here is a notion of chastening
rather than penalty. There may be other texts of Scripture, just as
there may be passages in the writings of the Early Church, that
can be interpreted in terms of a penal understanding of the
work of Christ, but there is no necessity to interpret them in this
manner and, for a host of reasons, one must question the legitimacy of interpreting them in this way. It is one thing to take
away sin, it is another thing entirely to take away the punishment for sin; it is one thing to bear sin (1 Peter 2:24), it is another
thing entirely to bear the penalty for sin; it is one thing to be
made sin for us (2 Corinthians 5:21), it is another thing entirely
to be made to bear the wrath of God against sin on our behalf.

A penal understanding of the work of Christ on the Cross –
the notion that, on the Cross, the Father in wrath inflicts the
penalty for sin on the Son instead of on us – is problematic theologically, historically, morally, and biblically. Theologically it is
problematic since it implies a division in God, a division within
the eternal Trinity between the Father and the Son but, more

radically, a division in God's eternal nature, as if justice and love, wrath and mercy, were rival and competing aspects of God's nature. God is simple: he is not and cannot be divided in himself; if we perceive his attributes or perfections as distinct this derives from the limitations of our perspective rather than from any distinction within God's nature or any division within the persons of the Trinity.[8] Historically the idea is problematic since, despite regrettable and misguided confusion with Anselm's 'satisfaction' theory,[9] I am aware of few clear and explicit references to this penal interpretation of the atonement until the late Medieval period.[10] A notion of justice is rather differently conceived in the Old Testament than in Aristotle and, as the Western Church developed, a notion of covenant law (*Torah*) appears to have been displaced by Roman law (*Lex*) and later Saxon law; a notion of punishment as inherent consequence or as a chastening and purging gives way to a notion of arbitrary penalty; a notion of penance as a demonstration of penitence leading to restoration gives way to a notion of penance as penalty for post-baptismal sin; a notion of purgatory as ultimate cleansing similarly gives way to a notion of extended penalty for post-baptismal sin; and penal understandings of Christ's Cross come to dominate and displace earlier understandings of the atonement.[11] Morally the idea is problematic, most obviously through the apparent injustice of one person bearing the penalty for another, but more subtly, as John Owen (1616–83) demonstrates, a notion of penal substitution necessarily leads either to a doctrine of universal salvation or to a doctrine of limited atonement since it would be unjust for the Father to inflict the same penalty for the same sin both on his Son and on the offender; either all are freed from this penalty by virtue of Christ's death or Christ bears the penalty for some but not all.[12] Owen's logic is compelling – which must lead one to question his premise since a doctrine of limited atonement, as espoused by Owen, leads again to questions concerning the unity and simplicity of God. But, most simply, this penal understanding of the atonement is biblically problematic: though so many biblical texts are marshalled in its support not one of them bears close scrutiny.

It is commendable that Christian theology should aspire to be systematic, that the Church should strive to expound doctrine in a manner that is internally and externally consistent and coherent – but systems are beguiling and all too easily come to displace those sources from which they derive. Beware of any system of theology that comes to be used as a lens and filter through which to strain the narrative of Holy Scripture. Beware of any system of theology that rests on proof texts with little reference to the narrative context in which they occur or to the broad sweep of the manner in which God is rendered in those narratives. Beware of any system of theology that expresses itself in a series of supposedly biblical shibboleths as markers of orthodoxy. It is not a little ironic that those who question penal understandings of Christ's Cross are dismissed as challenging Scripture's authority when the matter would appear to be entirely the other way around: an apparently pagan notion of penalty has come to be the lens through which Scripture is interpreted and understood.

Famously Gustav Aulén,[13] who also draws attention to this penal turn, concludes that the predominant understanding of the atonement in the early years of the Church's development focused on the Cross as Christ's victory, a victory over sin, a victory over corruption, a victory over death, a victory over the devil and elemental spiritual forces. Aulén's thesis can be challenged with respect to the manner in which he traces this penal turn in the Western Medieval Church, but it can similarly be challenged with respect to the conclusions he draws from his analysis of understandings of the atonement within the Early Church. In the first place, a victory over sin, a victory over corruption and death, and a victory over Satan and spiritual powers are sufficiently distinct to resist being comprehended as a single theory. But rather more significantly, an understanding of the atonement commonly referred to as 'the glorious exchange' was arguably at least as prominent within the Early Church as these various interpretations of Christ's victory. Following on from Paul's assertion that 'God made him who had no sin to be sin for us, so that in him we might become the righteousness of

God' (2 Corinthians 5:21), and the later and similar statement that '...though he was rich, yet for your sakes he became poor, so that you through his poverty might become rich' (2 Corinthians 8:9), together perhaps with the confession at the beginning of John's Gospel that through the one who becomes flesh amongst us we who believe become children of God, Irenaeus (c.130– c.202) concludes that the eternal Son became what we are so that he might make us what he is,[14] while Athanasius (c.297–373), rather more boldly, attests that he became human so that we might become divine.[15]

The problem with penal theories of atonement is not that they claim too much but that they claim too little, and that little which they do claim is shrouded in a suspiciously pagan notion of punishment as penalty. Paul's claim that Christ was made sin for us, that he became poor for us, suggests a far more radical and comprehensive identification. The eternal Son becomes wholly what we are: the one who is truly God assumes human flesh, the one who is sinless is made sin; the incorruptible bears our corruption; the immortal dies our death; the one who is the judge takes our place as the judged, bearing entirely the consequences of our sin and corruption, sharing our forsakenness, dying our death.[16] The cry of abandonment that Jesus cries is nothing less than our cry of abandonment: his cry is the cry of the child murdered by Herod's soldiers; his cry is the cry of the abused slave; his cry is the cry of the woman being raped; his cry is the cry of terror from the gas chamber; his cry is the cry of despair from the one contemplating suicide; his cry is the cry of lament from the psalmist; his is the desolation of every man and woman. Every human cry of despair is unique and particular – the particularity of individual suffering is not abolished at the Cross – but every human cry of despair is echoed in his cry, he enters fully into our desolation, our sin, our pain, our abuse, our dying, our death; he becomes what we are that we, through his entering into this desolation, might become what he is, the true humanity that is our destiny and calling.

Nor is this event merely and exclusively the work of the Son: earlier in the passage where he speaks of the Son being made sin for us, Paul affirms that it was God who, in Christ, was reconciling the world to himself (2 Corinthians 5:19); God is not in any sense divided in this drama; the event of the Cross is an act of God in which Father, Son, and Spirit are wholly united. Moreover, the event of the Cross is one through which we and the world are reconciled to God – there is no mention here (or, indeed, anywhere else) of God needing to be reconciled to us. God is not divided. Unequivocally, the Cross is an act of God's grace and mercy. In the person of the Son and in the power of the Spirit God himself makes our case his own; in the Son and by the Spirit he assumes and absorbs our sin and its consequences in order that we might be liberated into a true participation in his life by the Spirit. This is the glorious exchange: this is the possibility of our participation in him through his participation in us; this is the possibility of our righteousness through his being made sin; this is the possibility of our enrichment through his embracing of our poverty,

The dynamic of this glorious exchange, of course, is no more explicit in the passion narratives of Matthew and Mark than is a notion of penal substitution, but the former (unlike the latter) is explicit elsewhere in the New Testament and may therefore more validly and authentically be taken as a means through which Christ's cry of abandonment might be heard and interpreted. In both Matthew and Mark the immediate consequence of Jesus' death is the tearing of the Temple curtain. As several commentators note,[17] Mark's Gospel begins at the baptism of Jesus when the heavens are 'torn open', the Spirit descends, and the Father speaks, affirming the Son (Mark 1:9ff.). Now at the Cross, the Father is silent, the Son gives 'up his spirit' (Matthew 27:50), and the Temple curtain is torn in two (Mark 15:38; cf. Matthew 27:51) – are we perhaps to notice these contrasts between the Father's speaking and the Father's silence, between the Son receiving the Spirit and giving up his spirit, between the heavens opened to the Son and the Temple now opened to us? At his baptism Jesus identifies with repenting sinners and, in this respect, his baptism anticipates his Cross – are we therefore intended to notice these contrasts? There is some dispute concerning whether the curtain referred to should be understood as the curtain separating the Holy Place from the Holy of Holies or the curtain separating the court of the Temple from the Holy Place.[18] The focus on the 'outsider' throughout Matthew's Gospel – a focus signalled in the opening genealogy, represented by the Magi who travel to Bethlehem, reinforced by the relative prominence within the Gospel of women and of Gentiles, and concluding with the more positive response of the women on resurrection morning – could be heard as indicating that the outer of these curtains is to be understood: through the death of Jesus all may have access to fellowship with God, Jew and Gentile, male and female, slave and free; all nations may now become Christ's disciples.[19] But whichever of the curtains is intended the significance is surely similar: through Jesus' death a boundary and barrier between us and God has been removed; we have a possibility that previously was closed to us. Matthew's Gospel alone mentions an earthquake and the 'raising' of 'the bodies of many holy people' (Matthew 27:52f.). The reference is remarkable, not least for its absence in the other Gospel accounts. Perhaps the reference signifies the eschatological outcome of Jesus' death, this provisional 'raising' anticipates the final resurrection of the dead that issues from Christ's crucifixion – though we would more readily (and quite properly) assume the final resurrection to be an outcome of Jesus' resurrection than of his death – but maybe in this strange and isolated reference we have an allusion to a 'glorious exchange': it is through his death that we are brought to life; through his cry of abandonment we are brought into a new intimacy with God.

And maybe in the tearing of the Temple curtain (and perhaps in the earthquake and this provisional resurrection) we have some indication not just of the manner in which the giving of the Son's life is a 'ransom' but also of the manner in which this death is a bearing of sin. Our default assumption is to think of 'sins' rather than of 'sin', to think of the things which we have done which we should not have done (together perhaps with specific things which we should have done and have omitted to do) rather than the disposition and disorientation that under-lies those failures; to think of particulars rather than of a general context and condition. To interpret the Cross in terms of penalty, of course, reinforces this focus on the detailed and particular: a penalty is imposed in relation to a particular transgression (usually with a quite arbitrary relationship to that transgres-sion). When Paul speaks of death as the 'wages of sin' (Romans 6:23), when God warns Adam that he will die if he eats from the tree of the knowledge of good and evil (Genesis 2:17), that death is an inherent consequence rather than an arbitrary and imposed penalty. The story of Adam's fall is the story of one who, through disobedience and through grasping to be 'as God', is evicted from Eden and excluded from intimate commu-nion with God. And to be shut out of the garden is to be denied access to the tree of life, to be excluded from God's presence is to die.[20] There is nothing arbitrary in this consequence: to turn from God is to turn away from life and the source of life, it is to turn to corruption and death; this is certainly a 'judgement' – it was the decree of God within the story – but it is not an arbitrarily imposed penalty.

Significantly, John's Gospel speaks of Jesus as 'the Lamb' who takes away 'sin' rather than 'sins': he deals with the under-lying condition rather than merely with its symptoms, manifes-tations, and outcomes. In being made sin for us, by assuming our flesh, by identifying with us as sinners, by sharing in our suffering, despair, and desolation, Jesus takes not just our sin but he takes us as the sinners that we are into his death; he puts us and our sin to death; our deeply rooted disorientation and estrangement from God is crucified in him – and the outcome, for him and for us, is resurrection, is participation in his inti-macy with the Father, is the abolition of every barrier veiling us from God's presence.[21] To read the story of Jesus' crucifixion and cry of abandonment through the lens of a 'glorious exchange' is neither forced nor artificial.

Moreover, to interpret this drama in this way is to reinforce a paschal understanding of the Last Supper and of the elements of bread and wine with which Jesus there identifies. As at

Passover the people of Israel identify themselves as those who were redeemed from Egypt – as their participation in the elements of that meal are a means of participating in that distant drama – so in Holy Communion (as also in Holy Baptism) we are brought by the Spirit to participate in Christ and in his sacrifice; we participate through the Spirit in the drama of Good Friday in the hope of Easter Sunday. The crucified Christ is our Passover lamb, as he came to participate wholly in us and to identify with our sin so we, through bread and wine, truly participate in him and in his sacrifice; we are brought to identify with him as he identified with us; we celebrate an intimacy with God that was bought at the price of Christ's intimacy with us and identification with our sin. In Holy Baptism we are identified as the sinners for whom he died, by the Spirit we enter into his death and burial, we declare them to be our own in hope of a sharing in his resurrection by the power of the Spirit. In Holy Communion we celebrate this identification and participation again and again, we declare him and our participation in him as our true identity, we anticipate the fulfilment of that intimacy with God into which he has brought us.

The suffering of Jesus on the Cross was particular and specific, purposeful and meaningful; he achieves there what no other could achieve; his death there is a ransom, a Passover offering that opens to us a new intimacy with God. But his suffering and death are only particular and meaningful inasmuch as they are a genuine and profound sharing in our general and human suffering, inasmuch as they are a sharing in the meaninglessness and purposelessness of our suffering, inasmuch as they are a sharing in our disorientation, despair, and abandonment. To recognize Christ's suffering as specific and uniquely effective is not at all to detract from its human reality and depth – it is only because his suffering is truly human, only because his cry of abandonment is truly desperate, that he truly takes our place, that he truly is made sin for us. His cry of abandonment is uniquely his own, but it remains a true echo of our unique cries of abandonment, of my unique cry of abandonment.

And maybe, in counterpoint to his echoing of my cry of abandonment, I might come to perceive my cry of abandonment as an echoing of his. Every human cry of abandonment is unique and the sheer meaninglessness of most human suffering is a key element in this common sense of desperation – I am not suggesting any lessening of this sense of meaninglessness and desperation any more than I am suggesting any lessening of the desperation of Christ's cry of abandonment. But just as the significance of Christ's death is a direct outcome of the reality and depth of his abandonment, so perhaps, under the shadow of his Cross, our common suffering can gain significance without prejudice to its immediate inherent meaninglessness.

As noted earlier, just as the book of Jeremiah offers us some insight into the cost of being a prophet, so Paul's second letter to the Corinthians offers similar insight into the cost of being an apostle. In the course of the letter Paul recounts not just a catalogue of his sufferings, hardships, and afflictions, but also his ineffective pleading with God and even his sense of despair. If the letter really is to be understood as Paul's sustained response to the shallow triumphalism of some so-called apostles, then it would be entirely invalid to moderate or qualify the reality of his suffering in any respect. Yet even here Paul recognizes the treasure in the jar of clay (2 Corinthians 4:7ff.), the grace that is perfected even in his weakness (2 Corinthians 12:9).

More intriguingly (and enigmatically) Paul writes to the Colossians of filling 'up in my flesh what is still lacking in regard to Christ's afflictions, for the sake of his body, which is the church' (Colossians 1:24). How are we to understand this extraordinary claim? What possibly can be 'lacking in Christ's afflictions'?

In one sense, of course, there is and could be nothing lacking in Christ's suffering and it would be unthinkable and incoherent for Paul to suggest otherwise. Christ's suffering, like all human suffering, is uniquely his own, unique to the person that he uniquely is, and as uniquely his (as I have tried to argue) Christ's suffering is uniquely purposeful and effective precisely through the authenticity of his abandonment. Yet Paul has come to a place where he can only comprehend his own life, its joys and sorrows, its successes and failures, as included in and defined by the life of Christ. That we are now 'in Christ' is overwhelmingly Paul's preferred way of speaking of Christian disciples: to be part of the Church is to be part of Christ; to be baptised is to enter into his death and resurrection, is to put off an old life and to be clothed in Christ; to participate in bread and wine is to participate in his body and blood. Just as it would be unthinkable, therefore, for Paul to imply that Christ's sacrifice was in some sense deficient, it would be similarly unthinkable for Paul to view any aspect of his life as other than enclosed and included in the life of Christ through the Spirit. A significant proportion of Paul's suffering as catalogued in 2 Corinthians is specific to his calling as an apostle – he suffers persecution, opposition, and rejection, he endures abuse, beatings, and imprisonment – such suffering truly is for the sake of Christ's Church and, as such, it can readily be recognized as a participation in his suffering, a reiteration and echo of Christ's unique and uniquely purposeful suffering in the life of Paul. But not all Paul's suffering, I suspect, was specific to his calling. His reference to the willingness of the Galatian Christians to tear out their eyes to give to him, together with his gratitude for the manner in which they welcomed him despite his 'affliction' (Galatians 4:14f.), strongly suggests some physical illness or disability, and I remain unconvinced (and unimpressed) by attempts to interpret his 'thorn' in the flesh (2 Corinthians 12:7) as other than a physical affliction. Paul perceived not just his service as an apostle but the entirety of his life as caught up and included in Christ; the suffering he knew that was human and commonplace, as much as his specific suffering as an apostle, was therefore to be viewed as included in Christ and in Christ's suffering, weaknesses that could be the means of God's glory.

The eternal Son becomes our humanity, our sin, our suffering, our forsakenness, before God; his unique suffering uniquely includes, echoes, and reiterates all human suffering. Correspondingly, then, all human pain, suffering, and abandonment, like all human sin, can be recognized as included in his pain, suffering, and abandonment; all human frustration can be tempered with hope; all human suffering can be recognized as the birth-pangs of a new creation (Romans 8:18ff.); every cry of forsakenness can be an echo and reiteration of his cry of forsakenness. To perceive our human suffering as a participation in Christ's suffering does not render that human suffering any less real or devastating any more than the inclusion of our suffering in Christ's suffering renders his suffering any less real or devastating: the meaningfulness of his suffering does not render our otherwise meaningless suffering as meaningful, but it does orientate the meaningless in the meaningful. When, like the psalmist, I cry out in forsakenness I do not cry out alone, I cry out in him, and though my cry like his cry might be met with silence, under the shadow of his cry I can know that this silence is not the end of the story; like the psalmist but now under the shadow of Christ's Cross, I might yet come to be able to confess his faithfulness, even in the continuing silence and darkness.

You took my place that night in the garden
alone; with blood drop tears soaking the ground
as you prayed there; wrestling with the right,
the pathway none would choose; dread fate;
abandonment – yet confidence in one still
present, though seemingly absent, like friends
asleep.

You took my place: betrayed, deserted; now
rough soldiers bearing torches, cudgels, swords,
but that same compelling temptation to resist, fight back,
with friends, well meaning but misguided,
striking, confounded, fleeing. And one friend,
so trusted, now beguiled and beguiling, offers
a kiss.

You took my place: falsely accused and ridiculed,
persistent questions from those with no desire to listen;
provoking, mocking, ridicule. And by the fire
one true companion, denying in angry confusion
and fleeing shamed into the night. You stood
alone, more resigned than deviant, meeting accusation with
silence.

You took my place: not the nails or crown of thorns –
the implements of torture I've been spared –
but the crushing darkness, the cry of desolation,
the loneliness of stark abandonment, more
destructive than any earthquake or piercing spear.
You bore that darkness, absorbing hell wholly
for me.[22]

Chapter Seven

Darkness and God

And when the centurion, who stood there in front of Jesus, heard his cry and[1] saw how he died, he said, "Surely this man was the Son[2] of God!"

(Mark 15:39)

However we interpret this Roman soldier's confession as it is recorded in Matthew and Mark, whether (from his presumably pagan background) he is confessing Jesus as generally 'divine' or whether he is confessing him as *the* Son of God, the confession is astonishing and humanly inexplicable. In Matthew's account, alongside the darkness and the tearing of the Temple curtain, there is an earthquake marking Jesus' death, but in Mark's Gospel there is no earthquake, just darkness and the rending of a curtain which, more likely than not, the centurion would not have witnessed.[3] All he witnessed was the death of a man on an inexplicably dark day. All he heard was a cry which he at least could not have been expected to comprehend. Even if the significance of his confession is minimal – Jesus is an angelic being, one of the 'gods' come to earth – it is nonetheless extraordinary. In Luke's Gospel the confession is rather less remarkable: the one being crucified has forgiven his executioners and comforted a dying criminal – not, I suspect, common responses in those being put to death – perhaps understandable justification for the acknowledgement that 'this was a righteous man' (Luke 23:47). Both in Matthew and Mark, of course, the centurion's confession falls in a narrative context where we are continually surprised by those who recognize Jesus (and, perhaps, by those who don't). In Matthew's Gospel it tends to be the outsiders rather than the insiders who recognize Jesus: even when the risen Christ appears to his disciples at the conclusion of the Gospel we are told that 'some doubted' (Matthew 28:17). Mark, who begins his Gospel with unequivocal affirmation, '. . . the gospel about Jesus Christ, the Son of God', continues with Jesus rejected by religious leaders and recognized by the demon-possessed, with Jesus urging secrecy on those who have been healed: maybe this confession of the centurion echoes the confession with which the gospel began and stands in deliberate contrast to the fear of the women who are subsequently told of Christ's resurrection.[4] John, at the conclusion of his Gospel, is explicit in his aim, these things '...are written that you may believe that Jesus is the Christ, the Son of God, and that by believing you may have life in his name' (John 20:31), but, though less explicit, the other three Gospel writers have similar purpose, they simply have different strategies for establishing their point. And maybe the centurion's confession is key to the strategy of Matthew and Mark: albeit by quite different means, all four Gospel writers confront us with the claim that Jesus is the Son of God and Matthew and Mark do so in the context of a cry of forsakenness.

As noted previously, by ignoring the surprisingly impersonal form of Jesus' cry, 'my God . . .' rather than 'Father . . .', we can move too quickly to the implications of his deity without pausing sufficiently to give due weight to his humanity – the previous two chapters have been an attempt to redress that imbalance – but the centurion's confession and the overall thrust of the Gospels compel us to the issue of his deity: the one who cries out in God-forsakenness, the one who dies and is buried, is not only truly human, he is also truly divine. Here, perhaps in its starkest form, we are confronted again with the tension expressed at the Council of Chalcedon: the one who cries out to God in truly human God-forsakenness is himself truly God without prejudice to his true humanity. But the question is not just this Christological question of how this true man can be truly God, it is also the focused theological question of how God can be truly identified in this human cry of God-forsakenness. What might the word 'God' mean if God is defined in the Cross of Jesus, in a cry of dereliction, in God's apparent absence?

That the one who suffers and dies is truly God as well as truly human is not without appropriate qualification, but there are valid and invalid means of qualifying the confession and, as more generally with questions of Christ's true deity and true humanity, the Church has sometimes struggled with the recognition that the one who truly suffers is truly God.

In the first place (and with the least controversy) we should remember that it is specifically the Son, rather than the Father or the Spirit, who suffers, dies, and is buried – both the confession with which Mark's Gospel begins and this perhaps ambiguous confession on the lips of the centurion specify Jesus as 'son' – but the Son is only ever the Son in relation to the Father and the Spirit.[5] It is not the Father or the Spirit who becomes incarnate – though the incarnation of the Son only happens by their will and agency. It is not the Father or the Spirit who grows, learns, and matures within common and particular human limitations – though the development of the incarnate Son is in relation to the Father by the Spirit. It is not the Father or the Spirit who is baptised, identifying with repentant sinners – but, at his baptism, Jesus is identified as the Son in relation to the Father and the Spirit. It is not the Father or the Spirit who teaches, ministers, and works miracles – though each of the Gospels (and John's Gospel most thoroughly) clarify that all that the Son says and does is in relation to the Father and the Spirit. It is not the Father or the Spirit who is tried, tortured, abused, and crucified; it is not the Father or the Spirit who dies and who lies silent in the tomb until Easter morning – but, as in every other particular of the Son's incarnate life, we cannot consider the Son's passion other than in relation to the Father and the Spirit, albeit here in their felt and apparent absence. The Son is identified as the Son specifically in relation to the Father and the Spirit: the suffering of the Son is particular to his particular person but this cannot be without prejudice to the Father and the Spirit; who the Son is and what the Son does is ever and always in relation to the Father and the Spirit.[6] In this first respect, then, we cannot say without qualification that God suffers and dies on the Cross – it is the particular person of the Son who suffers and dies on the Cross – but the Son who suffers and dies is ever and eternally the Son only in relation to the Father and the Sprit; the Son's death, though particular to his person, must nonetheless be defining of God in God's Triune relatedness.

Secondly, and more directly venturing into the tensions of the Council of Chalcedon concerning Christ's true deity and true humanity, it is the incarnate Son who suffers, dies and is buried: the suffering of Jesus is the suffering of the eternal Son, the second person of the Trinity, but this suffering is specific to his incarnate life; he can and does suffer as he does only because he has come truly to share our humanity; his suffering, as the eternal person that he is, is nonetheless human suffering. Though certainly not uncommon in the Latin tradition of the West, the qualification that Christ suffered *in his human nature* became the key device in the Eastern Church for preserving the impassibility of God through the events of Christ's passion.[7] The conviction that God is impassible, incapable of suffering, dominated the development of Christian doctrine in the Early Church and was assumed virtually without question in both East and West until relatively recently. The expressed intention was not (and is not) to deny at all that the eternal Son truly suffers, but his suffering is specific to his humanity; he can and does only suffer because he is truly human and this human suffering is without prejudice to the impassibility of his divine nature.[8] Within this framework of understanding it is hard not to conclude that Christ's human nature and divine nature effectively function as tools, available to his single person as appropriate; in his incarnation, the human nature is available to the eternal Son as the means through which he can suffer and die without prejudice to the impassibility of his divine nature. This is a neat qualification, but perhaps it is rather too neat and too convenient: does this strategy really avoid Chalcedon's stricture that these two natures concur in Christ's single person '. . . without division, without separation'? How does the notion that Christ dies in his human nature (but not his divine nature) differ from Nestorius' apparent claim that Christ was born of Mary in his human (rather than divine) nature?[9] And ought we to note the irony that those who most vehemently sought to preserve Christ's divine nature from suffering were among those who most vehemently condemned Nestorius' distinction concerning his conception and birth?

Beneath and behind both qualifications, that it is the Son rather than the Father and the Spirit who suffers and dies and that the Son suffers and dies in his human nature, lurk suspiciously Greek notions of God's impassibility and immutability – God, by definition, cannot suffer and cannot change, he is the unmoved mover that moves all creation while remaining unmoved; the Son alone must suffer, and that in his human nature alone since the non-incarnate Father and Spirit, together with the divine nature of the incarnate Son, remain beyond and above suffering and change. Whatever the sources for this assumption within the Early Church (a matter to be discussed later in this chapter) it remained the assumption of both the Eastern and Western Church, largely in this form and virtually unchallenged, until the second half of the nineteenth century. Within the Western Church this assumption of an immutable God is demonstrated in what became standard representations of the Trinity: the Father, usually seated on a throne and staring impassively, holds a cross towards us with a dead or dying Son fastened upon it, while the Spirit in the form of a dove hovers between the two figures (almost invariably the figure of the Father in such depictions is significantly bigger than the figures of the Son and the Spirit). Ask anyone to point to God in this portrayal and almost invariably they will point to the figure on the throne rather than to the figure on the Cross or to the dove – the picture resolves the Trinity into the simple and immutable deity of the Father while limiting (if not obscuring and denying) the full deity of the Son and the Spirit; God offers the crucified

Christ to us and breathes out the Spirit, but God himself remains unmoved and impassive in the process.

Adolf von Harnack (1851–1930) is usually credited with being the source of the contemporary conclusion that developments of doctrine within the Early Church were vitiated with presuppositions deriving from Greek philosophy. As the twentieth century proceeded the assumption that these Hellenistic presuppositions had been formative for the development of doctrine and that this influence was generally a bad thing became commonplace, it has achieved the status of virtual orthodoxy, and it has led, in particular, to a series of reassessments of the significance of Christ's Cross for an understanding of God in relation to human suffering.

Probably most famously Jürgen Moltmann, in his book *The Crucified God*, argues that the Father and the Spirit must be involved together in the suffering and dying of the Son (albeit differently and distinctly) and that, therefore, (contrary to the tradition) God suffers and is changed in the process of that suffering – indeed, were God to be incapable of suffering and change he would be incapable of love.[10] Alongside and in coherence with this radical rejection of divine impassibility Moltmann expounds distinctive understandings of the relations of the Trinity, of God's relatedness to the world, and (at least by implication) of God's relatedness to time – this is not the occasion to analyse or respond to these ideas in any thorough or sufficient manner, but Moltmann's account is far from unproblematic. If love implies suffering and change what might this in turn imply for the eternal love of the immanent Trinity (the love of Father, Son, and Spirit before, beyond, and without the world)? Or has Moltmann's account left it difficult to speak of the immanent Trinity or of God before, beyond, and without creation? And if God is changed in encounter with the world might not this again imply that creation is necessary to God for God to be fully who he is or who he is becoming? The tendency of Western theology to resolve a doctrine of the Trinity in terms of God's oneness issues in the equally unacceptable alternatives of thinking of God as remote from the world or of thinking of God as, at least to a degree, identified with the world.[11] The apparent irony in Moltmann's thought is that a thorough and careful doctrine of the Trinity should issue in the possibility of simultaneously affirming God's distinction from creation and intimate involvement within creation but, for this reader at least, this potential is never fully exploited in Moltmann's developing work. There is always the lingering suspicion of a creation that contributes to God's Godness, of a God who is, in some respects, dependent upon creation and creation's development.

As mentioned already, Moltmann is by no means alone amongst contemporary Christian theologians to challenge the notion of God's impassibility and immutability – what is perhaps surprising given the centrality of the Cross for the gospel story is that such notions passed largely unchallenged for so long – and at least some of these other thinkers offer (in my view) rather more nuanced and cautious discussions than that of Moltmann,[12] but there remain weighty reasons to challenge this entire contemporary theological trend, nuanced or otherwise.

In the first place, while the immediate concern of this book is with human suffering and the presence (or absence) of God in and with the experience of human suffering, we must beware lest we reduce Christ's suffering to a general and non-specific suffering, losing sight of its particularity. It was the argument of the last chapter that Christ's suffering has particular effect precisely because it is an authentic sharing in our general human suffering, but Christ's suffering is nonetheless particular and with particular effect. His dying cry of forsakenness, though echoing the general, is specific and unique. His death is reconciling in a way that could be true of no other death. His death cannot be reduced to enacted sympathy,[13] and neither does it serve as a dramatic means of justifying God to us in the context of our suffering. This contemporary focus on questions of how God in Christ suffers with us might easily lose sight of the truth that here uniquely he suffers for us.[14]

Secondly, this contemporary focus on the implications of Christ's Cross for God's relatedness to suffering could easily be heard as culturally patronizing with respect to previous eras of the Church. Moltmann writes consciously and confessedly under the shadow of Auschwitz, responding to the unspeakable horrors of the holocaust, horrors that since have been mirrored in the death camps of Stalin, the killing-fields of Cambodia, and in repeated attempts at genocide and 'ethnic cleansing' in the name of a vicious nationalism. But are we really to presume that previous ages of the Church were without their own horrors, cruelties, and afflictions? European wars throughout the Middle Ages were notoriously brutal before we begin take account of the terrors of plague. The years through which the Early Church developed its doctrine were years of persecution and the sadism of the Roman arena. The twentieth century, for all its ruthless depravity, has no monopoly on suffering and pain; ours are not the first generations to cry out in felt God-forsakenness – the psalms of lament anticipate our questionings and generations of Christian thinkers who maintained this strange notion of divine impassibility were no less oppressed by the questions of human suffering. To speak and to write as if our context uniquely forced these questions upon us is crass, pompous, and historically naïve. Rather than tacitly assume that previous generations of the Church, by their weddedness to a notion of impassibility, were responding inadequately to the problems of human suffering perhaps we should listen to them a little more intently before concluding that they were swept along by a Hellenistic (and therefore pagan) notion of God's nature.

Which leads thirdly to the (I hope) non-patronizing assumption that Irenaeus and those who followed his instincts in this respect were not idiots and were all too aware of the manner in which the gospel story challenged many of the suppositions of Hellenistic philosophy.[15] Certainly it is possible to argue that some thinkers within the Early Church – Clement of Alexandria (c.150–c.215), Origen (c.185–c.254), or Evagrius (345–399), for example – were somewhat seduced by aspects of inherited Greek thinking (though even these examples can be and have been disputed), but the work of Irenaeus and Athanasius (by way of contrasting example) is marked by frequent criticism and qualification of their common Hellenistic heritage. Similarly, Thomas Aquinas (*c.*1225–1274) – probably the most formative thinker in the Western Medieval Church – for all the influence of Plato and Aristotle in his work, shows little reluctance to dispute with them when their ideas conflict with his reading of the Scriptures and of the Christian tradition. Irenaeus continually repudiates every Hellenistic hint that questions the essential goodness of the material creation, and Irenaeus repeatedly confesses the truth of Christ's deity and the reality of his suffering, yet Irenaeus retains this strange notion of divine impassibility, straining language to speak with apparent contradiction of the genuine suffering of one who is truly impassible:

> ...thus He took up man into Himself, the invisible becoming visible, the incomprehensible being made comprehensible, the impassible becoming capable of suffering, and the Word being made man, thus summing up all things in Himself: so that as in super-celestial, spiritual, and invisible things, the Word of God is supreme, so also in things visible and corporeal He might possess the supremacy, and, taking to Himself the pre-eminence, as well as constituting Himself Head of the Church, He might draw all things to Himself at the proper time.[16]

Surely (and finally), in response to this straining of language, we should ponder why such writers, so concerned to respond faithfully to Scripture even at the expense of their Hellenistic heritage, should cling so tenaciously to this apparently contradictory notion of divine impassibility. For Moltmann, suffering implies change and this plainly is our common human experience: it would be strange indeed for anyone to experience pain, abuse, or distress of any kind without being affected by that experience; I am who I am by virtue of years of clinical depression not to mention other significant experiences that have shaped me; my hearing of the psalms of lament and of the narratives of Christ's Cross inevitably is influenced by who I am and how I have been affected and formed through experience. But can we really assume that God's involvement in creation's history affects him and shapes him as it shapes us? What might it mean for God to be eternal; to be involved in time and space without being qualified or determined by time and space; to be 'the same' from age to age? Maybe these early Christian writers are reminding us that God, even in his intimate involvement with us, remains the One who is also transcendently other than us; that a confession of God's changelessness is also an aspect of Scripture's witness to the nature of God, albeit differently expressed and always held in tension with the genuineness of God's engagement with the world.

A prayer of Moses the man of God.

Lord, you have been our dwelling place
    throughout all generations.
Before the mountains were born
    or you brought forth the earth and the world,
    from everlasting to everlasting you are God.
You turn people back to dust,
    saying, "Return to dust, O mortals."
For a thousand years in your sight
    are like a day that has just gone by,
    or like a watch in the night.
    (Psalm 90:1–4).

Any careful reader of the Old Testament should not be taken wholly by surprise by the Gospel narratives of Christ's incarnation. Throughout the narratives of the Old Testament the God of Israel is never reduced to a detached and distant observer of Israel's history: he walks and talks with Adam in the garden; he turns up for lunch at Abraham's tent, he meets with Moses at a burning bush; he leads his people by cloud and fire; he fills Tabernacle and Temple with his glory; he makes himself known to judges, priests, prophets, and kings; though perhaps unrecognized (or unacknowledged) he works his covenant purposes through the problematic stories of very ordinary people, through Rahab, through Naomi and Ruth, through the prayers of Hannah.

He is ever and always intimately involved in his creation and in the unfolding and often erratic history of his people, but he is so as the one he uniquely is.[17] God's involvement with his people is never qualified but neither is his eternal nature. Over and again we are reminded, as in Psalm 90, that God is God, he is 'from everlasting to everlasting', he is unchanging, faithful, constant. In Psalm 22, similarly, the recitation of God's past faithfulness to his people is the first confession of the psalmist in the context of his distress – albeit a confession that, initially at least, does not seem to relieve his anguish. Sometimes, as in Irenaeus, the narratives of the Old Testament strain language to maintain this tension of God's intimate involvement and God's distinctness: 'He who is the Glory of Israel does not lie or change his mind . . . the LORD was grieved that he had made Saul king over Israel' (1 Samuel 15:29, 35). The phrases here translated 'change his mind' and 'grieved' are the same word in Hebrew,[18] as the King James Version puts it: 'the Strength of Israel will not lie or repent . . . and the LORD repented that he had made Saul King'. Here, as everywhere, God is intimately involved in the unfolding story, but he is so as the one he is, as one who is different to us, as one who is utterly faithful to his covenant purposes, as one who will not be compromised or manipulated by our sin and sinfulness: it is precisely God's constancy and faithfulness that, in the flow of the narrative and of Israel's history, issue in his 'change of mind' concerning Saul.[19] In so many respects these narratives, not least because they are *narratives*, portray an entirely different image to that of the static, immoveable, dispassionate abstraction that was postulated in Hellenistic thought – but the one encountered in these narratives is nonetheless unchanging, utterly faithful, never reduced (and certainly not enhanced) in his involvement with us and with his creation.

Could it be then that it was this changelessness of faithfulness, this living constancy, that impressed itself on the thinkers of the Early Church, that rendered them reluctant to dispense with the notion of divine impassibility, albeit (as in Irenaeus) re-conceiving the notion in the light of the gospel story? This seems to be the conclusion of Thomas Weinandy in his robust

response to contemporary dismissals of the notion of impassibility:[20] the fathers of the Early Church were not enshrining a
notion of God as static, immobile, and dispassionate, but were
maintaining a confidence in God's living constancy; God is
unchanging not because he is uncaring or unloving but rather
he is unchanging because he could not be more caring or more
loving than he eternally is; he is impassible, not because he is
dispassionate or apathetic, but rather because he could not
possibly be more passionate.

Whether or not Weinandy is right in his analysis of the Early
Church fathers,[21] it must be conceded that, for some Christian
thinkers over the centuries, an impassibility of abstraction, of
immobility, of detached otherness, has dominated and obscured
the livingness of God's faithfulness in the biblical narratives. In
response to such abstractions the reaction of Moltmann and
others is understandable albeit, I suspect, mistaken. A more
appropriate response to this hermetically sealed notion of God's
otherness surely would be an affirmation of his intimate
involvement with us and with his creation that did not implic-
itly prejudice his covenant constancy. What is required is a more
attentive listening to the narratives of Scripture while resisting
the temptation to resolve its inherent tensions in one direction
or the other. What is required is an ever more thorough commit-
ment to allow the gospel story to determine our understanding
of the eternal God.

Karl Barth, the Swiss theologian who died in 1968, is justly
honoured for the extraordinary insight and radical freshness
of so much of his theological contribution but, with others, I
suspect that his treatment of the doctrine of God and of God's
perfections is his most perceptive and formative legacy.[22] Here
Barth, repudiating every hint of Hellenistic abstraction, determines to interpret God's nature resolutely in response to God's
self-revelation in Christ: who God is here he is eternally; theology is a 'thinking after' (*Nachdenken*) God's self-revelation in
Christ. God's changelessness, therefore, is not an immobile
detachment but a living constancy. God is the one who loves in
freedom: his freedom is not indeterminate, it is specifically the

freedom of his eternal lovingness revealed in Christ, but his love remains free, it is never necessitated or determined by that which is other than God, it is his love, it is grace. The incarnation and crucifixion do not constitute a change in God, they rather are defining of who God is eternally as Father, Son, and Spirit.

The prayer of Jesus recorded in John 17 speaks of the love between Father and Son 'before the creation of the world' (John 17:24): God is love in all eternity in the eternal communion of Father, Son, and Spirit; he does not need creation in order to be loving; he does not need us in order to be loving; he does not need creation or us in order to be who he eternally is. But we only come to know that this is who God is eternally because it is revealed to us in the gospel story; because this eternal communion of love between Father, Son, and Spirit has been enacted in our history, because the eternal Son has taken our flesh and lived among us. Jesus begins this prayer by speaking of the glory he had with the Father 'before the world began' (John 17:5), but here, as elsewhere in this Gospel, Christ's glory includes the Cross; the Father glorifies the Son through the Cross and not despite the Cross. If we are to take the revelation which is the gospel story seriously, if we are truly committed to a theology which is a 'thinking after' these narratives, then we must allow the event of the Cross, together with every other aspect of the gospel story, to be wholly defining of our understanding of God. With Moltmann and others we must confess that the Cross of Jesus determines our understanding of the nature of God, but perhaps contrary to Moltmann and others we must further confess that this event implies no change in God, it is rather revealing and defining of who God eternally is; that God in the flesh of Christ suffers and dies here is an unveiling of God's authentic eternal nature.[23]

Where Moltmann and others (following Barth) are justified in their protest is in response to our common tendency to bring presuppositions about God's nature to the gospel story, adjusting our hearing of it in order to make it conform to our presuppositions. If we come to the gospel story assuming that God is detached and dispassionate in relation to all that is not God we will have no alternative but to strain the gospel story through this filter. But surely the assumption (for assumption it is) that the events of the gospel imply some form of change in God similarly betrays an assumption that, before and beyond the gospel story, God is other than as he is defined here? Perhaps (with Barth) we need to listen to the gospel story even more radically than Moltmann, allowing it to dethrone our presuppositions, allowing the story to be wholly defining of our understanding of God: there is no change in God here – God is eternal, beyond all change – this rather is a rendering in our history of who he eternally is.

The glory of Christ revealed through the Cross is precisely the glory he had with the Father 'before the world began'. This is not to say that the Son suffers in all eternity – though the suffering of the Son in the flesh is taken up into the eternal life of God and we should not too quickly dismiss verses that speak of Christ as 'the Lamb that was slain from the creation of the world' (Revelation 13:8). But it is to say that the human suffering of Christ in the flesh is an outworking in our history of the active, living, and wholly passionate love of God in eternity. There is no change in God here, there is rather a revelation of his eternal nature, an historical and narrative rendering of who he unchangeably is.

The standard (and only legitimate) representation of the Holy Trinity within the Eastern Church illustrates the story of Abraham's three visitors (Genesis 18:1–33). Probably the most famous example of the icon is that by Andrei Rublev (c.1360–1427/30): the three angels are portrayed as neither male nor female; they are virtually identical with one another; they are in an attitude of mutual submission. Unlike the typical Western depiction of the Trinity, they are clearly in relation to one another, in communion with one another; they are seated around a table and a chalice filled with wine sits at the centre of the table. Moreover, the shape of the chalice is reproduced in the shape between the three angels seated at the table. The 'shape' of God is the shape of an eternal covenant and communion between Father, Son, and Spirit; an eternal love that binds these three eternal persons in one indivisible eternal nature. The Cross of Jesus, the entire gospel story, the entirety of God's story with his people narrated in Scripture, is simply the outworking in our time and space of this eternal covenantal nature of the Triune God; who he is in this story he is eternally. It is not that God eternally suffers anymore than it is the case that God is eternally merciful or wrathful, it is rather that suffering, like the perfections of wrath and mercy, is an outworking of God's eternal nature in our time and space, in the context of our sinfulness and creation's fallenness. God is not eternally wrathful or merciful; wrath and mercy are outworkings in our history of his eternally simple nature, outworkings of the eternal covenantal love between Father, Son, and Spirit in response to human sin, weakness, and suffering. But God responds to human sin and creation's fallenness not merely in wrath and mercy, but ultimately in the Son's taking our flesh, being made our sin, suffering and dying with us and for us that we, through this sheer act of merciful identification, might come to participate again in communion with God, might become truly human as the Son is truly human. In the Rublev icon there is space at the front of the table; we are invited to share in this communion; the perspective of the painting draws us into the picture.

It would be extraordinary for us to assume that the centurion at the foot of Christ's Cross recognized all this. But maybe it wouldn't be extraordinary to assume that the Gospel writers recognized all this and included the centurion's confession to make precisely this point. The purpose of the Gospels, albeit differently established, is to present Jesus as the Christ, as the Son of God – but in pursuing this aim, knowingly or unknowingly, the Gospel writers are implying a radically distinct definition of the being and nature of God: God is such as can assume our humanity in the person of the Son and, in that assumed humanity, can assume our sin, can share our suffering, and can die in our place – this does not imply some change in one who from age to age is changeless, rather it is an historical and narrative defining of who this one is changelessly from age to age. The crushing darkness, the bearing of abuse, the suffering, the dying, even the cry of abandonment, are not foreign to the nature of God but are the outworking in our history of who he is eternally: 'Jesus Christ is the same yesterday and today and forever' (Hebrews 13:8). As the narratives of Matthew and Mark reach their conclusion a Roman soldier witnesses an execution, is overwhelmed by darkness, hears a cry of God-forsakenness, and concludes, inexplicably, that there is that here that is godlike. We cannot escape the conclusion that, in the narratives of these two Gospels, God is identified in suffering, dying, darkness, and even a cry of abandonment.[24] These Gospels reach their conclusion in a seemingly impenetrable contradiction: God is recognized and thereby defined in apparent God-forsakenness – to the disarming implications of this uncomfortable conclusion we must finally turn.

Dear Lord,
our lives are blighted by presuppositions about who you are,
about what you can and cannot do,
about where you are present and where you are absent.
The story of Christ's Cross obliterates our presuppositions:
you can do what you have done;
you are present even when everything seems to speak of your absence.
Please give us the grace, like that centurion,
to recognize you in the darkness and the contradictions;
to discern your presence even in our own cries of forsakenness.
For the sake of him who was forsaken for us.
Amen.

Chapter Eight

Darkness and Presence

Truly you are a God who hides himself,
O God and Saviour of Israel. (Isaiah 45:15)

I was sitting at the bedside of a woman dying of cancer – being
with the dying is one of the deepest honours and privileges of
pastoral ministry and I have sat similarly on many occasions,
but this occasion haunts me not least for my poor handling, not
of the dying, but of the understandable anger of this woman's
daughter who could only view this dying as God's failure: God
had let down her mother; he had deceived her; his promises had
come to nothing. It was probably barely a year earlier that the
mother had joined the church where I was pastor. She was
already very sick. She came to us from another church in the
area where she had been encouraged to believe that God would
heal her cancer to the point of being discouraged from seeking
any medical help. By the time she came to us her sickness was
beyond medical cure (and, of course, may have been so from the
beginning). I too believe that God heals people, but I believe
he usually does so through the gifts of medical science and,
beyond the ministrations of those human gifts (in my very
limited experience), he doesn't seem to heal people very often.
Such otherwise inexplicable healing, when it occurs, is a miracle,
something extraordinary, something beyond the ordinary and
everyday, something that points beyond itself to a future yet to
be fulfilled. I'm certainly not suggesting that we shouldn't pray
for healing – we most certainly should, just as we also should be

open to those created means through which God generally mediates such healing – but we should pray for healing always remembering that we inhabit a fallen world; neither we nor the creation of which we are a part are yet as God ultimately wills; sickness suffering and death are ever threatening aspects of present reality; the death rate remains at one hundred percent. Besides which we should also recall that Jesus has some disarming things to say about those who continually seek 'signs' (Matthew 12:39) and one wonders how then we have arrived at a point where this woman's story could occur in this form, where some spiritualities appear dominated by the expectation for miraculous signs. Probably the greatest pastoral responsibility is to prepare men and women to die – a responsibility rendered all the more difficult to fulfil in a context where death is effectively denied and perceived as defeat, where immediate physical healing is presumed and virtually demanded.

There are now (and probably have always been) notions of faith that are difficult to distinguish from presumption: forgiveness and healing come to be perceived as rights to be claimed rather than merciful provisions to be sought in prayer; health, wealth, and happiness displace holiness and humility as the marks of authentic discipleship; meek assurance is misconceived as a heavenly insurance policy; the Cross of Jesus comes to be viewed as the basis on which we can hold God to account rather than the place at which, in Christ's humanity, he holds us to account; God's gracious covenant is reduced to a bargaining contract; the Holy Spirit is reduced to an automaton. Given the catalogue of thwarted hopes that issue from this pseudo-gospel it may seem amazing that it remains beguiling – but the world is full of sad and suffering people sufficiently desperate to struggle towards any mirage of comfort and hope. Such distortions derive from a myopic reading of Scripture: the psalms of lament are either ignored or are marginalized as belonging strictly to an older dispensation; the book of Job is read solely in the light of its 'happy ending'; Jesus' promise of a hundredfold return in this present age is welcomed but the qualifying addition of 'persecutions' is ignored (Mark 10:30); Jesus' claim to have overcome the world is trumpeted, but his warning that in this world we will continue to have trouble is passed over in dismissive silence (John 16:33). Anyone subscribing to this parody of the gospel has but two possibilities when longed for blessing or healing fail to materialize: either their faith has failed or God has failed – and in either direction lies despair.

That human faith has failed remains the common and far too slick refuge of at least some of those who peddle this cruel and false creed – cruel since it amasses guilt and spiritual inadequacy on those already suffering; false since its focus is on our human effort and achievement rather than on the merciful and patient grace of God. Faith itself is a gift of the Spirit, it is not a human achievement. That which God does in our lives, by way of forgiveness, restoration, renewal, healing, and ultimately resurrection, is wholly his gracious work, received by us but in no sense achieved by us. Before this gracious God we can only stand spiritually helpless and wholly dependent. All that we receive from him is sheer gift, an overflowing of his eternally gracious nature, it is neither merited nor earned. Which, of course, invites the alternative possibility: God has failed; the one who is presumed to have promised health, affluence, and happiness has failed to deliver – and in this desperate conclusion lies the most profound despair.

It was this despair that gripped an excusably angry young woman at her dying mother's bedside; it is a despair that, sadly, I have encountered over and again, sometimes with equal vehemence; it is a despair that leads some to turn away from God, not realizing that they had been duped with a wholly false vision of God in the first place. Faith is trusting God in the darkness, it is not a quasi-magical means of turning the darkness into light. It's not that I don't believe that God can and does turn darkness to light – ultimately he will, but here and now he calls us to trust him, even in the darkness. Like Daniel's three friends standing before Nebuchadnezzar (Daniel 3:17f.), we believe that God can turn darkness to light, that he can act miraculously to change us and our circumstances, but even if he doesn't we will still trust him. Faith is no more a magical power than it is a feeling; faith is a settled trust in God even in the continuing darkness and silence, even when we cannot see and cannot hear. Such trust, of course, is not exclusive of expressions of despair, but this is the despair of afflicted trust rather than the despair of distrust and denial. Job, Jeremiah, the psalmists, all cry out in the despair of trust rather than distrust: it is precisely because they trust God that they turn to him in lament, complaint, and renewed appeal; the despair of distrust doesn't issue in lament, it issues in the silences of denial and rejection. To be truly biblical, to be shaped by the narratives and prayers of Scripture, is to be shaped in a manner that admits the possibility of a sustained darkness and a corresponding despair of trust, it is not to be shaped in a manner that denies the possibility of a sustained darkness and issues in a corresponding despair of distrust.

The predictable and somewhat bemused atheistic rejoinder to this trustful despair would be to dismiss such as fanciful and entirely pointless delusion. What possible point can there be in continuing to trust in one who remains silent in response to anguished prayer and allows darkness, pain, abuse, and suffering to continue? Is this despairing trust any more than the torturous perpetuation of a pointless myth? What in reality is the difference between a 'God' who remains silent and inactive and no such 'God' at all? Or, as Wisdom's parable of the invisible gardener puts it 'how does what you call an invisible, intangible, eternally elusive gardener differ from an imaginary gardener or even from no gardener at all'?[1] It may be churlish to respond that atheism itself has problems of coherence: can it ever be coherent dogmatically to deny that which one cannot define? Even if darkness and despair were unremitting and unrelenting one would still need to account for the continuing existence of physical reality, the seemingly innate sense of rightness and wrongness, of good and evil, the advent, persistence, and resilience of the Christian Church, the historical claims of the Christian gospel. Nonetheless, were the sustained darkness and the corresponding trustful despair to be the unrelenting testimony of Scripture or the entirety of Christian experience the objection and dismissal might have purchase – but this is far from the case.

One of the concerns of this book has been to draw attention to Psalm 22 as an example of the psalms of lament, to affirm its poignancy for common experience, and to urge the inclusion of such psalms in personal devotion and corporate worship. The concern is personally motivated and arises in response to the creeping marginalization of these psalms in Christian worship. But the psalter is not unremitting lament; if approximately one third of the psalms are laments this leaves two thirds of the psalms that are not laments, that are celebrations of thanksgiving, of praise, and of worship. The Old Testament is candid in its accounts of human tragedy and despair, but by no means is this the whole of the story: over and again God acts in mercy to deliver his people; year upon year Abraham and Sarah struggle with the frustrations of childlessness yet they also experience significant material prosperity; Joseph languishes in slavery and prison, betrayed by his brothers and falsely accused before his master, yet even in prison he flourishes and, on release, he is raised to govern Egypt. The stories of oppression, such as those of Elijah and Jeremiah, are balanced by the prospering of David and Solomon; stories of affliction and hardship more often than not come to resolution. At times the apostle Paul despairs of life but he also knows contentment; he pleads that the thorn in his flesh might be removed but he also is an instrument for the healing and transformation of many. Good Friday gives way to Easter morning. God sometimes is silent – this remains the focal theme for this book – but he is not always silent, time and again he acts in deliverance and healing. In the first two chapters of this book and subsequently I have tried to be open about my own struggles with depressive illness and the perspective that this inevitably has given to a hearing of Scripture and particularly to a hearing of the psalms of lament, but my life is not unremitting depression: I am blessed with a loving wife, the friendship of my children, the delight of my grandchildren, and with material provision far exceeding the expectations of my youth; I too would testify to answered prayer, to extraordinary acts of healing, to a felt sense of the presence of God. My purpose in writing this book is not at all to deny or to belittle felt experience or tangible blessing – I gladly rejoice in both – but my purpose is to admit that felt experience and tangible blessing are sometimes absent and to caution against ever founding faith and discipleship on such occasional and provisional evidences. Contrary to atheistic objections, Christian faith is not lacking in rational coherence and empirical evidence – but to focus on such, at least in any personal sense, is probably to miss the point.

The Bible witnesses to God's revelation of himself in our human history, as noted above, this witness encompasses stories of failure and stories of flourishing, stories of want and stories of abundance, stories of abuse and stories of deliverance, stories of sickness and stories of healing, stories of death and stories of resurrection – but for Christian faith the story of Christmas, of Good Friday, and of Easter Sunday is focal and ultimately defining, every other story of Scripture (and, indeed, every other human story whatsoever) is viewed through this lens. God speaks and acts in human history, but once in human history God fully enters our human history in the person of Jesus of Nazareth; his eternal Word assumes our flesh; his eternal Son assumes our nature. He bears our sin, endures our abandonment, and dies our death in order that we, by sharing in his resurrection life, might become truly and fully the men and women he calls us to be, participating by the Spirit in his relatedness to the Father, sharing in the life of God. Beyond every other Scriptural story, beyond every other human story, it is this story that is ultimately defining of who we are and of who God is. And at the climax of this story, for the Gospel writers at least, God is defined and recognized in human suffering, dying, and death, in darkness, in a cry of God-forsakenness. At the very centre of Christian faith we encounter the seemingly impenetrable paradox that God is most profoundly present and active in his apparent absence; that the one who is truly human is never more truly divine than when he cries out in darkness and abandonment; that God is to be known here, in darkness, abandonment, dying, and death, or he is not to be truly known at all; that who he is in this desolation is who he truly and eternally is. This Cross and this cry of forsakenness stand in human history as the decisive and total repudiation of the sham of triumphalism, of every specious, shallow, and costless spirituality – the event of this desolation is the authentic majesty of the one who is truly God. It is not that God is not truly known in acts of healing and deliverance, in visions and prophecies, in felt experiences of his presence, it is rather that the narrative of the Cross suggests that he is most truly and profoundly known in suffering and death, in darkness and silence, in the despair of felt abandonment – this is his authentic glory; this is the mystery of his most focused presence; this is his ultimate self-revelation.

And this paradoxical theme that is the climax of the Gospel narratives seems to be echoed throughout the narratives of Scripture: when God makes covenant with Abram he does so in the context of 'a thick and dreadful darkness' (Genesis 15:1–21); for Jacob to see the face of God is to wrestle with a man until daybreak and to be left with a limp (Genesis 32:22–32); for the people of Israel, if not for Moses, Mount Sinai was a place of darkness and fear (Exodus 19:1–25, Deuteronomy 5:24–29; cf. Hebrews 12:18–21); for Elijah, the LORD was not present in wind, earthquake, and fire, but in a crushing silence (1 Kings 19:11f.);[2] for Ezekiel, the glory of the LORD is present, no longer in the Temple, but with the exiles in Babylon (Ezekiel 1.1f.); for the psalmist, the LORD takes delight, not in sacrifices and offerings, but in 'a broken spirit, a broken and contrite heart' (Psalm 51:16f.); and later the apostle Paul, wrestling with God over his thorn in the flesh, is told that God's 'power is made perfect in weakness' (2 Corinthians 12:9). The text with which this chapter begins appears without any obvious connectedness to the verses that immediately surround it – almost interrupting the poetic flow of prophecies concerning Cyrus, concerning Israel's restoration, concerning the future disgrace of those who worship idols, we find this aphorism that God is one who hides himself. Yet maybe this seeming aside is the most pertinent response to the central chapters of Isaiah in their entirety. Both here and over and again in Israel's history God's presence is hidden in the unexpected, the confounding, the mysterious. What could be more puzzling than that God should be present with his people in exile, that he should designate a Persian King his anointed, that he should restore this defeated, shamed, powerless, and stateless people to the land of his promise? Over and again in Scripture God hides himself in the very dynamic of making himself known.[3]

Moreover, if the hiddenness and strangeness of God's presence is a recurring theme of Scripture, so too are poverty and suffering recurring themes of Christian discipleship: Jesus identifies those who are blessed as those who are poor in spirit, who mourn, who are meek, who are hungry and thirsty for righteousness, who are merciful, who are pure in heart, who are peacemakers, who are persecuted and insulted (Matthew 5:1–11); those who would follow him are warned that, unlike the foxes and the birds, he has nowhere to lay his head (Luke 9:58); those who would sit at his right and left in the coming kingdom are asked whether they can share in his baptism and his cup (Mark 10:35–40); we are warned that, as he is persecuted, so we shall be persecuted (John 15:20f.); we are told that, if we would come after him, we must deny ourselves, take up our cross, and follow him (Mark 8:34). For those who first heard these words of Jesus they had an all too literal significance: to take up one's cross was not merely a challenging metaphor but was more immediately a most disturbing prediction; several of those first disciples were to die a torturous death as the consequence of their faithful discipleship; this would be the fulfilment of their sharing his baptism and his cup. For subsequent generations and for some still today this call to discipleship continues to be no mere metaphor; to be baptised in some contexts is still to invite persecution and death. But, as far as we know, one of those disciples who was specifically told he would share Christ's baptism and Christ's cup died peacefully in old age – to take up one's cross cannot be restricted to a literal outcome, though neither can that literal outcome be excluded even for those of us whose discipleship at present attracts little physical threat; to take up one's cross must also signify a more general and comprehensive sharing in Christ's suffering.

If the argument of chapter six of this book is correct, if Christ's death is not merely a bearing of a penalty but a bearing of sin, a becoming of who we are in our sinful and fallen condition and context, then our more general sharing in Christ's Cross, since it is actually our cross in the first place, is inevitable. Inasmuch as we have not yet come fully to share his resurrection we continue to share in his Cross which, in fact, is his sharing in our cross. His suffering uniquely delivers us from an ultimate suffering of an ultimate separation from God – the Temple curtain has been torn in two – but here and now his suffering does not deliver us from the suffering that is common to humanity, it reinterprets it but it does not necessarily nullify or diminish that suffering. Moreover, that the call to discipleship comes in the form of a call to take up a cross reinforces the inevitability, the appropriateness, and the necessity of our present sharing in his suffering. In the light of his suffering we can come to understand our suffering differently, as a sharing in his suffering, but this insight does not render the pain less painful, the sense of forsakenness less desperate.

And if it is Jesus' cry of God-forsakenness that takes us to the heart and depth of his suffering, then the heart and depth of our suffering as a sharing in his suffering may well also take form in the despair of apparent God-forsakenness. The tendency and temptation for us would be to view our sense of abandonment as spiritual failure – either we have failed God or God has failed us – but to interpret our sense of abandonment through the lens of Christ's Cross, not to mention the repeated experience of God's people in Scripture and in Christian history, is to recognize our sense of forsakenness as an inevitable, appropriate, and perhaps even climactic aspect of our spiritual journey – the true God is never more present and active than in his apparent absence and silence. Paradoxically, the experience of apparent God-forsakenness, rather than apparent health, wealth, and happiness, is a mark of authentic discipleship. Generally, a spiritual journey is not unremitting despair, there are green pastures, quiet waters, and periods of restoration, but it is often in the valley of the shadow of death that, perhaps contrary to felt experience, God is most profoundly present,[4] and it is often in the presence of enmity that we are overtaken by his surprising provision and renewal (Psalm 23:1–6). As I intimated in personal stories at the beginning of this book (stories that echo the overwhelming experience of God's people over the centuries), I can identify periods of darkness and despair as instances of significant growth and insight – God always and eternally is the one who perfects his strength in our weakness and is glorified in the human cross of one who trusts him. The despair of God-forsakenness, then, is an aspect of normal Christian experience, indeed, it may well prove to be the most formative aspect of normal Christian experience. This insight, of course, does not render the despair less desperate, the pain less painful, the darkness less oppressive, the silence less distressing – like the psalmist we may cry out in anguished confusion (God can take it and Scripture sanctions it) – but, whether we recognize it at the time or not, and even if the darkness and silence prove unremitting, God is always and eternally the God of the Cross, the God who is most acutely present and active in his apparent absence and silence, this is who he is, this is the mysterious and 'hidden' way that he makes himself known.

I am certainly not advocating a form of spiritual masochism – only a fool would seek this darkness of despair or wallow in it; no one longs for God's silence or apparent absence – but I am calling for a renewal of the recognition that the psalms of lament, echoed in the cry of Jesus, are spiritually normative, that periods of felt abandonment are not to be shunned or misconstrued as spiritual failure. Let us pray that this darkness doesn't engulf us, in any of its forms, but if and when it does let us not misconstrue it as spiritual failure or mistake our feelings of forsakenness for the reality. As in the case of Job, there is probably vastly more occurring here than we can possibly comprehend and certainly more occurring here than we can immediately perceive.

This analysis of the spiritual life with a positive evaluation of the experience of desolation echoes that which Christian tradition has generally termed the 'Dark Night of the Soul' – over the centuries a host of Christian writers have reflected on acute and sustained periods of spiritual darkness and silence and have concluded, as this book concludes, that such generally constitute the most profound and formative aspects of a spiritual journey. In this general analysis and positive evaluation the Christian tradition is overwhelmingly in agreement but the details of description and analysis vary significantly between the different writers. For this reason, though wanting to place this reflection firmly within this tradition, it is nonetheless necessary to distance what is being said here from some of the ways in which this 'dark night' has been expressed and discussed by some other writers.

In the Introduction to this book I mentioned that St John of the Cross distinguishes the soul's dark night from depression though, as I argued there, this derives from a rather different and restricted definition of depression before it signifies any different understanding of the soul's dark night. For St John of the Cross depression seems to be restricted to an early disillusionment, when the cost of true discipleship begins to dawn: it is a mark of immaturity rather than a mark and means of maturity. Of course it is the case that some Christians pass through such disillusionment and that this should be acknowledged as a symptom of immaturity rather than maturity – one could add that any spirituality that gives inadequate space to the psalms of lament and which promotes a triumphalistic cheapening of the Christian gospel actively encourages such immaturity – but to define this disillusionment as depression and to restrict a definition of depression to this form of disillusionment is unhelpful, or at least not the manner in which we today would define depression (we must beware of criticizing older writers without taking due account of their context and contextual assumptions). As I observed previously, not all that is properly defined as clinical depression is a form of what the Christian tradition has identified as the dark night of the soul and not every experience of the dark night of the soul would properly be identified as clinical depression. Inevitably and deliberately I have written as I have from the prospective shaped by my own journey, but my intention is not at all to universalize my own experience; for many an experience of desolation has no clinical root or implication.

But perhaps it is in his expression of the soul's dark night itself that I also struggle with St John of the Cross. For him, this darkness is the desolation consequent on an abandoning of all worldly cares and material things, a desolation of emptiness as the soul cleaves to God alone, a desolation in felt God-forsakenness precisely because every other possible source of hope and security has already been abandoned.[5] The first letter of John warns us not to 'love the world or anything in the world' (1 John 2:15) and some elements of the Christian tradition have tended to interpret the warning as grounds for a quite negative and world-denying asceticism. An asceticism of simplicity and contentment are to be encouraged as proper aspects of Christian discipleship[6] but we should guard against this degenerating to a world-denying spirituality that conflicts with a vibrant doctrine of creation. One element which marked Judaism and then Christianity as distinctive in the ancient world was a wholly positive view of creation: God is the creator of all physical reality and he declares that creation to be good (Genesis 1:1 – 2:3); the eternal Son is the one in whom, by whom, and for whom all things are created (Colossians 1:15–17); all things in earth and heaven are reconciled to God in him (Colossians 1:19–20). As we read through the stories of the Patriarchs and the visions of the Prophets we find time and again that God's blessing is expressed in material terms – a spirituality that simply opposes the physical and the spiritual is a distortion of the witness of Scripture. The desolation that has been the focus for this study is not the consequence of a world-denying asceticism, abandonment to God that is synonymous with an abandoning of all else. This desolation rather can overtake us in prosperity as much as in poverty, in health as much as in sickness. It is an overwhelming and crushing sense of God-forsakenness without prejudice to physical and material provision; it may come in the wake of physical or mental sickness, it may come in the wake of material deprivation, but this need not always be the case. More importantly, as noted above, it is not in any way sought or to be sought, it is simply not to be shunned or misconstrued.

Yet, notwithstanding these reservations, St John of the Cross articulates a darkness that has been articulated over and again by Christian writers, Catholic and Protestant. To find oneself in a spiritual desert is not the prerogative of any single expression of spirituality but is the common experience of generations of Christians, and, whatever his assumptions, St John of the Cross brings this desolation into clear poetic and reflective expression. However this dark night has been expressed and understood, it has been the common experience of countless Christian disciples who overwhelmingly, for all their distinctions, affirm this darkness as the most significant and formative element of their Christian journey. The circumstances or 'triggers' of this darkness may be various; its common element is the desolation of God-forsakenness, an echoing of the cry of the psalmist, an echoing of the cry of Jesus; and the common response of Christian discipleship is to endure this darkness, trusting in the presence of one who seems so utterly absent, allowing this darkness to shape and deepen trust rather than to undermine it.

Finally I can have no certainty concerning the nature of the depression that so often has engulfed me, the original clinical diagnosis may or may not be accurate, but it is in these terms that I have come to interpret it, in continuity with this tradition of the soul's dark night, in continuity with the psalms of lament, as an echo of the cry of Jesus. This recognition doesn't render the depression any easier to bear – as I confessed in chapter one, initially it entirely overwhelmed me, leaving me confused, doubting, and in grave danger of losing any sense of direction – but, with Paul, I trust the one who can perfect his strength even in my weakness and, with the benefit of hindsight, this has been the case over and again: Good Friday and Holy Saturday are torturous, long, and dark, but they are not unending and Easter morning dawns. I am what I am, and even in darkness and felt abandonment I will trust him.

And this, I suspect (but cannot prove) is what is occurring in Psalm 22 and in the sudden change of tone in verse 22. It remains possible, of course, that something has changed, that whatever is oppressing and threatening (whatever its nature) has been removed or has withdrawn, that the darkness has lifted, that the apparently absent God has revealed his presence – but, other than the change of tone in this verse, there is nothing in the text to suggest such transformation. It is at least equally possible that nothing has changed, that oppression and threat continue, that the darkness is unrelenting, that the sense of God's absence is unrelieved – but, notwithstanding circumstances and felt abandonment, the psalmist will trust God and will express that trust in confession and praise. Faith is not a feeling, nor is it a magical incantation that turns darkness to light: faith is trusting God even without feeling and even in continuing darkness; faith is faithfulness. Once in human history the one who is truly human and truly God cried out in pain, in darkness, in felt abandonment; his cry met with silence, death, and a borrowed grave; for the whole of the second day there was silence, a Sabbath of apparent decay, disillusioned and despairing disciples; Easter morning had been predicted but it was nonetheless a surprising reversal. His suffering and abandonment changes everything – the curtain is torn in two – but, for now, our suffering and sense of abandonment continue, continue until the reversal of the final Easter morning.

> The cockerel crowed this morning as before;
> and, though strangely interrupted, this day
> the sun rose, and shines brightly still; nor
> do children, despite rebuke, cease their play;
> men turn familiar steps to Sabbath prayer –
> the hollow echo of a cold tradition –
> while scribes and priests continue unaware
> there's none to hear their customary petition.

God is dead – we killed him yesterday:
religious leaders, shamed by pure integrity;
provincial governors scared to confront the fray;
and erstwhile friends, in cowed complicity,
deserting, denying, and life betraying
for such a little price, thirty pieces
of silver, the price of one's enslaving,
for with his death all hope of freedom ceases.

Cold in the tomb his tortured body lies
stretched, scarred, deformed by crucifying pain,
his rotting flesh – a fetid feast for flies
and maggots – women and noblemen in vain
anoint this lifeless cadaver: he's dead –
messianic justice and hoped for peace must pale
and rot with him, entombed, stone-sealed, close-guarded;
here all expectations of God's kingdom fail.

And so no point in lingering at his tomb
or pondering what might have been had he
not died. Let us now quit this upper room,
and memories of all we hoped that we could be.
Spare us these myths of empty graves and angels,
of phantom gardeners – mere wishful tales told
by those rejecting cold reality for fables.
Tomorrow, bound for home we walk the Emmaus road.[7]

Concluding Reflection

> He then began to teach them that the Son of Man must suffer many
> things and be rejected by the elders, chief priests and teachers of
> the law, and that he must be killed and after three days rise again
> (Mark 8:31).

It's the 'must' in the sentence that is troubling: the Son of Man
must suffer . . . Why? Is there some inexorable necessity in suffering – ours and his – or is suffering merely inevitable, a tragic
consequence of creation in its present and persisting state? Both
possibilities issue in a repeated 'why?' Whether suffering is a
necessity of creation or merely an inevitability of creation, why
should this be the case; why might God have imposed such a
necessity or created the universe in such a manner that suffering
is inevitable; could not God have created the world some other
way, some way whereby pain and suffering, sin and evil were
excluded as possibilities? The last way of putting the question at
least identifies that some forms of human suffering are self–
inflicted: sin implies a sinner; abuse implies an abuser; torture
implies a torturer. This identifies the wilful nature of some suffering but it doesn't explain the 'accidental'; it doesn't explain
what is usually termed 'natural' evil (which more properly is a
way of identifying some evil as inherent in creation itself); it
doesn't explain the cruelty that seems characteristic of animals,
birds, fish, reptiles, and even insects; it doesn't explain human
sickness; it doesn't explain mental illness.

Scripture poses this question 'why?' over and again but offers no clear and decisive answer. Surprisingly, not even the sin of Adam is ever clearly identified within Scripture as the source and reason for the suffering that pervades creation. Christian theology has often been less hesitant: all suffering is an outcome of the 'Fall', which was not just humanity's fall but the fall of all creation – which may well be correct but which postulates beyond what is scripturally plain; which does not explain why human sin should have this cosmic effect; which does not straightforwardly explain why creation seems to have been vitiated with suffering and pain long before the advent of men and women or the possibility of human sin; and which, more particularly, personally, and pastorally, does not begin to explain or to satisfy the problem of particular suffering, of why this man or this woman should suffer in this way. Surely it is the particularity of suffering that is the most pressing problem: suffering doesn't seem to be evenly distributed; some people seem to endure more than their fair share; the sheer unfairness of it all is part of the problem.

Resisting the temptation to offer explanation, to engage in philosophical hair-splitting over the distinctions between a necessity and an inevitability, between different forms of necessity, even between different forms of suffering, we can only conclude that this is simply the way it is; creation suffers; we suffer; this is how it has always been; the question is not 'why me?' but 'why not me?'. Except to conclude with such resignation is more stoical than biblical: Scripture may not offer any clear explanation of suffering, any refined theodicy defending God against charges of injustice, but Scripture abounds with protest, with the complaints of Job, the prayers of Jeremiah, the psalms of lament. There is no resigned stoicism here – there is complaint. And while the question 'why?' is certainly not absent from these laments it doesn't predominate: alongside the questions of why this has happened are questions of why God appears to have abandoned us to suffering, where is God at the point of our deepest need: 'why have you forsaken me'?[1] The ease with which we succumb to a false piety of quiet resignation or a triumphalistic and deluded denial of suffering's reality is as foreign to Scripture as is the justification of theodicy. Scripture is disarming in its honest protest. Scripture laments. If we would be truly biblical, truly shaped by these narratives, prophecies, and prayers, we would join in these laments, trusting God enough to honour him with our honesty, our complaint, our distress. The sons of men and the daughters of women suffer – that's the way it is – but we don't suffer in silence, we suffer in prayer, we trust God sufficiently to join Job, Jeremiah, and the psalmists in lament.[2]

So much New Testament scholarship of the twentieth century was devoted to pondering the significance of the phrase 'Son of Man' on the lips of Jesus. Clearly it is a form of oblique self-designation but is it a deliberate avoidance of more common Messianic titles, is it an allusion to the eschatological figure in Daniel 7, or is it an echo of the phrase used in Ezekiel, does it refer to a particular eschatological figure or does it signify a representative of all men and women, might it even be reminiscent of the servant figure in Isaiah? These possibilities, of course, are not mutually exclusive: the phrase 'Son of Man' may be Jesus' means of avoiding explicitly Messianic titles but it may also be an eschatological reference and neither possibility need exclude a more simple representational reference. Jesus, as 'Son of Man', is simply man: certainly he comes as the eschatological man, the final man who sums up all humanity in himself, but precisely as such he is the representative man, standing in the place of all men and women throughout human history, re-presenting them in himself before God. Simply as man it is necessary or inevitable that he should suffer – all men and women suffer; all creation suffers; the Son of Man similarly *must* suffer. But as the 'final' man, the man who sums up all men and women in himself, the man who represents all men and women before God, it is appropriate that he too should suffer, not just sharing in the suffering that is common to us but somehow encapsulating that suffering, holding in himself every aspect of our human condition, and incorporating us, as the men and women we are in our fallenness and sin, by representing us before God. Out of inexpressible and eternal love for us he *must* suffer. His suffering is real as our suffering is real. His darkness, like ours, is unremitting. His cry of desolation is at least as desperate as ours. But unlike our suffering, his suffering – for reasons we may never fully comprehend – changes our human condition before God, a curtain is torn in two, God still may seem remote but he never will be, an ultimate separation from him has been abolished, the eternal Son has become what we are in order that we might become the true humanity before God that he is.

In Psalm 22 the psalmist cries out in apparent God-forsaken-ness but he also confesses God's faithfulness while possibly knowing no relief from his distress, no light in the darkness, no reassurance of God's presence, no break in the silence. Christ's cry of dereliction echoes the psalmist's cry but we know that his cry was not the last word, was not the end of the story. Our cries can similarly echo the psalmist's cry and, when we struggle to express our anguish, we can make his words our own – but we cannot pray his prayer without coming to his confession, and we cannot any longer pray his prayer without hearing it echoed in the cry of Jesus, without knowing that, as an outcome of his unique suffering, our suffering and distress cannot possibly be the last word. The Son of Man must suffer. We too must suffer – the world is not yet as God ultimately wills it to be; we are not yet as God ultimately wills us to be; the outcomes of Jesus' death are not yet wholly fulfilled. But, notwithstanding our felt abandonment, we do not suffer alone and our suffering cannot possibly be final or ultimate. The Son of Man *has* suffered and nothing, not even our despairing desolation, can ever be quite the same again.

Dear Lord,
thank you that once in history your Son took our place:
he shares our humanity;
he entered our suffering;
he died our death.
We still suffer;
we still die;
we still cry out in darkness, in anguish, in apparent
abandonment.
Please help us,
even in the darkness and the silence,
to know that the suffering, darkness, and silence are not the last
word;
to perceive our resurrection in his;
to hold on trustfully no matter what.
For the sake of him who rose from the dead.
Amen.

Notes

Introduction

1 John E. Colwell, *Living the Christian Story: The Distinctiveness of Christian Ethics* (Edinburgh: T & T Clark, 2001).
2 John E. Colwell, *The Rhythm of Doctrine: a Liturgical Sketch of Christian Faith and Faithfulness* (Milton Keynes: Paternoster, 2007).
3 Kathryn Greene-McCreight, *Darkness is my only companion: A Christian response to mental illness* (Grand Rapids: Brazos, 2006).
4 St John of the Cross, *The Collected Works of Saint John of the Cross*, trans. Kieran Kavanaugh and Otilio Rodriguez (Washington, DC: ICS Press, 1991), pp. 115–117.

Chapter One: Into The Darkness

1 Stephen Fry, *The Secret Life of the Manic Depressive* (two part documentary), Directed by Ross Wilson, originally broadcast by BBC 2 (2006).
2 Kathryn Greene-McCreight, *Darkness is my only companion*.
3 'In place of depression, Israel's form has petition, and here the forms are most to be contrasted. Depression is appropriate if the speech is monologic. But Israel's form is boldly dialogic, and the one who hears, or is expected to hear, is not addressed in hopeless despair but in passionate expectation.' Walter Brueggemann, *The Psalms and the Life of Faith*, ed. Patrick D. Miller (Minneapolis: Fortress Press, 1995), p. 91.
4 מידעי מחשך

Chapter Two: Reflecting on the Darkness

1 While it is by no means an easy read, probably the best exposition of Christ's humanity in these respects occurs in the work on the Holy Spirit by John Owen (the seventeenth-century Puritan): *A Discourse concerning the Holy Spirit* (1674) in *The Works of John Owen*, vol. 3, ed. W. H. Goold (London: Banner, 1965), pp. 159–188.

2 'For who even of slight intelligence does not understand that, as nurses commonly do with infants, God is wont in a measure to "lisp" in speaking to us? Thus such forms of speaking do not so much express clearly what God is like as accommodate the knowledge of him to our slight capacity. To do this he must descend far beneath his loftiness.' *Institutes* I xiii 1.

3 There are good reasons not to put 'an evil spirit from the Lord' in the same category (1 Samuel 16:14).

4 In part, the conflict between Pharisees and Sadducees exposes some resistance to this culture of spiritual understanding (Acts 23:8).

5 It is far from clear that passages of Scripture usually cited in support of this tradition have any such reference.

6 For instance, Matthew 8:16; 12:15; Luke 6:19.

7 For a recent discussion in this respect see Amos Yong, *Theology and Down Syndrome: Reimagining Disability in Late Modernity* (Waco: Baylor University Press, 2007).

8 '…sin is forgiven, not erased; Christ is raised but not "undead" so we can perhaps believe that disabilities are transformed, not eliminated…' Sally Nelson, *A Thousand Crucifixions: The materialist subversion of the church?* , *The Whitley Lecture 2009* (Oxford: Whitley Publications, 2009), p. 8.

9 C. H. Spurgeon, *The Soul-Winner* (London: Passmore & Alabaster, 1897), pp. 197–199.

10 It should be noted that Paul's weakness and vulnerability is an underlying theme in this entire letter and not just chapter 12.

11 It is for this reason that we must resist viewing Job as in any sense an 'answer' to the problem of suffering; cf. David B. Burrell, *Deconstruction Theodicy: Why Job has nothing to say to the puzzle of suffering* (Grand Rapids: Brazos, 2008).

12 Quoted by Christopher Howse in 'Sacred Mysteries', *Daily Telegraph*, 1 September 2007.

13 Letter to Charles Wesley on 27 June 1766, originally published in Telford's edition of the letters (1931), cited in Henry D. Rack, *Reasonable Enthusiast: John Wesley and the Rise of Methodism* (London: Epworth Press, 1989), p. 546.
14 John E. Colwell, *Promise and Presence: an exploration of sacramental theology* (Milton Keynes: Paternoster, 2005), p. 149.

Chapter Three: Darkness and the Psalmist

1 Or *Yet you are holy, / enthroned on the praises of Israel* (*NIV* margin).
2 Or / *I am laid* (*NIV* margin).
3 Some Hebrew manuscripts, Septuagint and Syriac; most Hebrew manuscripts / *like the lion,* (*NIV* margin).
4 Or / *you have heard* (*NIV* margin).
5 Hebrew *him* (*NIV* margin).
6 ὤρυξαν χεῖράς μου, καὶ πόδας
7 reading כרו instead of כארי
8 For a discussion of metaphor in the Psalms see William P. Brown, *Seeing the Psalms: A Theology of Metaphor* (Louisville: Westminster John Knox, 2002).
9 'As with other complaints in the Psalter, the reader is never sure what the real trouble is, and this is due primarily to the picturesque descriptions.' Konrad Schaefer, *Berit Olam: Studies in Hebrew Narrative & Poetry – Psalms*, ed. David W. Cotter, assoc. eds. Jerome T. Walsh and Chris Franke (Collegeville, MN: The Liturgical Press, 2001), p. 54.
10 'That is why the lament is, to a certain extent, a complaint against God. The abandonment comes from him; the refusal to help is his; he is to blame for his deafness to the cry of the suppliant.' André LaCocque, 'My God, My God, Why Have You Forsaken Me?' in André LaCocque and Paul Ricoeur, *Thinking Biblically: Exegetical and Hermeneutical Studies*, trans. David Pellauer (Chicago and London: University of Chicago Press, 1998), 187–209, p. 191.
11 Or *Yet you are holy, / enthroned on the praises of Israel* (*NIV* margin).
12 In the Hebrew text this first 'but' and the subsequent 'yet' are the same pre-fixed conjunction (in the Septuagint similarly the same simple conjunction is employed): in English translation

we have the possibility of inferring nuances of significance that could not be explicit in the ancient text.

13 μακρὰν ἀπὸ τῆς σωτηρίας μου οἱ λόγοι τῶν παραπτωμάτων μου.

14 כי־אתה גחי מבטן (𝔐); ὅτι σὺ ἐι ὁ ἐκσπάσας με ἐκ γαστρὸς (LXX)

15 For an extended discussion of Baptism and the difficulties of both the infant Baptism and the believer's Baptism stance, see my Promise and Presence, chs. 5 and 6.

16 'Saying "my God" is based as well on quite personal experience . . . Therein lies the pain. His statements about God are confessions of faith, of confidence in God. But in the prayer they serve also as complaints . . .'. James Luther Mays, Psalms Interpretation: A Bible Commentary for Teaching and Preaching, ed. James Luther Mays, O.T. ed. Patrick D. Miller Jr. (Louisville: Jonn Knox, 1994) p. 109.

17 'The theme of "the possibility, efficacy and reality of giving praise to God" runs through the whole psalm. Verses 22–31 do not indicate that the suppliant has yet experienced Yhwh's deliverance. They do indicate that the suppliant knows Yhwh will deliver.' John Goldingay, Psalms, vol. 1: Psalms 1–41, Baker Commentary on the Old Testament Wisdom and Psalms, ed. Tremper Longman III (Grand Rapids: Baker, 2006), p. 323; cf. 'What the psalmist now affirms is that God is present in the affliction' J. Clinton McCann, Jr. A Theological Introduction to the Book of Psalms: The Psalms as Torah (Nashville: Abingdon, 1993), p. 172; cf. 'D'ordinaire, dans les poèmes de ce genre, l'action de grâces anticipe sur la délivrance escomptée, à titre de promesse destinée, en dernier ressort, à provoquer le secours d'En-Haut. En est-il de même ici?' Louis Jacquet, Les Psaumes et le cœur de l'homme : Etude textuelle, littéraire et doctrinale, Introduction et Premier Livre du Psautier – Psaumes 1 à 41 (Belgium: Duculot, 1975), p. 516.

Chapter Four: Darkness and Israel

1 For probably the most sustained expression of this possibility see Aubrey R. Johnson, Sacral Kingship in Ancient Israel (Cardiff: University of Wales Press, 1967[2]).

2   See for instance John H. Eaton, *Kingship and the Psalms, Studies in Biblical Theology*, Second Series 32 (London: SCM, 1976), pp. 34ff., though note that Hermann Gunkel, in his *Introduction to the Psalms*, includes this psalm as a communal complaint song: Hermann Gunkel, *An Introduction to the Psalms: The Genres of the Religious Lyric of Israel*, completed by Joachim Begrich, trans. James D. Nogalski (Macon, Georgia: Mercer University Press, 1998). For a concise summary of attempts to root this psalm in the cult of Israel see André LaCocque, 'My God, My God, Why Have You Forsaken Me?', p. 193.

3   Sigmund Mowinckel, *The Psalms in Israel's Worship*, trans. D. R. Ap-Thomas, vol. I (Oxford: Blackwell, 1967), p. 235.

4   Sigmund Mowinckel, *The Psalms in Israel's Worship*, trans. D. R. Ap-Thomas, vol. II (Oxford: Blackwell, 1967), p. 8.

5   'Instead of placing the accent on the *Sitz im Leben* of the psalms within the cultus or among other concrete practices, literary analysis sets out in quest of a suprahistorical invariant, capable of being removed from the historical conditions of its first appearance and of being reinvested in new life contexts.' Paul Ricoeur, 'Lamentation as Prayer' in André LaCocque, and Paul Ricoeur, *Thinking Biblically*, 211–232, p. 214.

6   Artur Weiser, *The Psalms: A Commentary*, trans. Herbert Hartwell, The Old Testament Library, Gen. Eds. Peter Ackroyd, James Barr, John Bright, G. Ernest Wright (London: SCM, 1962).

7   'It is therefore more likely that the worshipper's prayer has already been granted than that he still anticipates even in prayer itself the future answering of his prayer and his future deliverance, This latter view is, however, held by most expositors.' Artur Weiser, *The Psalms*, pp. 224f.; cf. 'They [the lines] presuppose not that the suppliant must have *seen* the answer to the plea in vv. 19–21, but at least that the suppliant has *heard* it and has thus made a transition to the conviction that Yhwh has responded, and that deliverance is therefore a reality.' John Goldingay, *Psalms*, vol. 1: Psalms 1–41, *Baker Commentary on the Old Testament Wisdom and Psalms*, ed. Tremper Longman III (Grand Rapids: Baker, 2006), pp. 335f.; cf. 'We may be permitted to assume that by means of an "oracle of rescue" Yahweh bestowed answer and rescue on the lamenting poet'. Hans Joachim Kraus, *Psalms 1–59: A Commentary*, trans. Hilton C. Oswald (Minneapolis: Augsburg, 1988), p. 298; cf. André

LaCocque, 'My God, My God, Why Have You Forsaken Me?', pp. 187f.

8 For this argument at some length and in detail see my *Promise and Presence*.

9 Cf. Paul Ricoeur, 'Lamentation as Prayer', p. 221.

10 '. . . sometimes we are told in plain words that Yahweh puts more value on the psalm singing and the humble or grateful heart of which it is an expression than on the sacrifice of animals.' Sigmund Mowinckel, *The Psalms in Israel's Worship*, vol. II, pp. 90f.

11 In this respect see Walter Brueggemann, *Praying the Psalms: Engaging Scripture and the Life of the Spirit* (Carlisle: Paternoster, 2007²); cf. Fergus McDonald, 'Do the Psalms speak Today?', *Scottish Bulletin of Evangelical Theology* 26.2 (2008), 170–186.

12 For elaborations of this maxim see John Swinton, *Raging with Compassion: Pastoral Responses to the Problem of Evil* (Grand Rapids: Eerdmans, 2007) and Matthew Boulton, 'Forsaking God: A Theological Argument for Christian Lamentations.' *SJT* 55.1 (2002): 58–78; cf. André LaCocque, 'My God, My God, Why Have You Forsaken Me?', p. 189.

13 *The Baptist Church Hymnal: Chants and Anthems with Music* (London: Psalms and Hymns Trust, 1900); cf. *The Baptist Church Hymnal: Revised Edition* (London: Psalms and Hymns Trust, 1933). *The Baptist Hymn Book* (London: Psalms and Hymns Trust, 1962) included a selection of chants as an appendix.

14 A line from the second verse of the song 'Jesus, we celebrate Your victory', John Gibson, Copyright © 1987 Thankyou Music, P.O. Box 75, Eastbourne, East Sussex, BN23 6NW, UK.

15 For this interpretation of the letter see D. A. Carson, *From triumphalism to maturity: an exposition of 2 Corinthians 10–13* (Grand Rapids: Baker Book House, 1984).

16 *LW* 31, 39–70. For Martin Luther this focus upon the Cross and upon the hiddenness of God was a key Reformation theme, repudiating what he perceived to be presumptuous certainties of late Medieval theology.

Chapter Five: Christ's Human Darkness

1 Some manuscripts do not have *heard his cry and.*

2 Or *a son.*

3 For a brief discussion of the possibilities see W. F. Albright and C. S. Mann, *The Anchor Bible – Matthew: Introduction, Translation, and Notes* (New York: Doubleday, 1971), p. 350; W. D. Davies and Dale C. Allison, *A Critical and Exegetical Commentary on The Gospel According to Saint Matthew,* vol. III, *Commentary on Matthew XIX–XXVIII* (Edinburgh: T & T Clark, 1997), p. 624; a more detailed discussion can be found in Donald P. Senior c.p., *The Passion Narrative According to Matthew: A Redactional Study* (Leuven: Leuven University Press, 1982), pp. 295ff.

4 For discussion of this misunderstanding with respect to Elijah see W. F. Albright and C. S. Mann, *The Anchor Bible – Matthew,* p. 350; W. D. Davies and Dale C. Allison, *Commentary on Matthew XIX–XXVIII,* p. 626; Eduard Schweizer, *The Good News according to Mark: A Commentary on the Gospel,* trans. Donald H. Madvig (London: SPCK, 1971), pp. 353f. together with chapters three and five of Anthony J. Clarke's *A Cry in the Darkness: The Forsakenness of Jesus in Scripture, Theology, and Experience,* Regent's Study Guides 10, gen. ed. Paul Fiddes (Oxford/Macon: Regent's Park College/Smyth & Helwys Publishing, Inc., 2002). I am immensely grateful to Anthony Clarke, a friend and colleague, for his most helpful and thorough discussion of this text and its theological interpretation – discussion that continually informs the later half of this book.

5 So for instance: '[t]he critical question is whether Mark expects the reader to "fill in the gaps" and anticipate Jesus' vindication.' Rikk Watts, 'The Psalms in Mark's Gospel' in Steve Moyise & Maarten J. J. Menken (eds.), *The Psalms in the New Testament* (London: T & T Clark, 2004), 25–45 p. 43.

6 The earliest manuscripts of Mark's Gospel end abruptly with a preposition: καὶ οὐδενὶ οὐδὲν εἶπαν ἐφοβοῦντο γάρ.

7 '. . . it is perilous to argue from the use of one verse that Jesus was quoting the whole psalm; indeed, he may not have been quoting at all.' Leon Morris, *The Gospel according to Matthew* (Grand Rapids: Eerdmans, 1992), p. 721. While affirming that Jesus appropriates the text rather than merely cites it, Richard Bauckham nonetheless holds that Mark's broader allusions to

the psalm justify a reading of the cry 'in the context of the whole psalm'. Richard Bauckham, *Jesus and the God of Israel: 'God Crucified' and other studies on the New Testament's Christology of Divine Identity* (Milton Keynes: Paternoster, 2008), pp. 255f.

8 For a fuller but nonetheless accessible discussion of these distinctions and their proper complementarity see Tom Smail, *Once and for All: a Confession of the Cross* (London: DLT, 1998), pp. 19–28.

9 Joachim Jeremias, *The Eucharistic Words of Jesus*, trans. Norman Perrin (London: SCM, 1966); for a discussion of this see chapter seven of my *Promise and Presence*.

10 Ἀληθῶς οὗτος ὁ ἄνθρωπος υἱὸς θεοῦ ἦν.

11 Ἀληθῶς θεοῦ υἱὸς ἦν οὗτος. The use of the definite article in Greek is quite distinct to its use in English and the arguments concerning the proper translation of these phrases turns on issues of syntax that are less than certain.

12 Ὄντως ὁ ἄνθρωπος οὗτος δίκαιος ἦν.

13 See for instance Richard A. Burridge, *What are the Gospels? A Comparison with Graeco-Roman Biography* (Cambridge: Cambridge University Press, 1992) and *Four Gospels, One Jesus? A Symbolic Reading* (London: SPCK, 1994).

14 ὁμοούσιον τῷ πατρὶ κατὰ τὴν θεότητα, καὶ ὁμοούσιον ἡμῖν τὸν αὐτὸν κατὰ τὴν ἀνθρωπότητα (*consubstantialem Patri secundum deitatem, consubstantialem nobis eundem secundum humanitatem*).

15 κατὰ πάντα ὅμοιον ἡμῖν χωρὶς ἁμαρτίας (*per omnia nobis similem absque peccato*).

16 ἐν δύο φύσεσιν ἀσυγχύτως, ἀτρέπτως, ἀδιαιρέτως, ἀχωρίτως γνωριζόμενον (*in duabus naturis inconfuse, immutabiliter, indivise, inseparabiliter agnoscendum*).

Chapter Six: Christ's unique darkness

1 Some manuscripts *Eli, Eli*.

2 Or *a son*.

3 'The cry of dereliction has been used by the early Reformers in defense of the view that Jesus on the cross endured "in our place" God's judgment on sin, even that the words from the cross alludes [sic!] to the despair of the damned, whose

torment Jesus would have suffered in his soul . . . No correct interpretation will adhere to this perspective.' Leopold Sabourin, S. J., *The Gospel According to St Matthew*, vol. 2 (Bombay: St Paul Publications,1982), pp. 915f.

4 νῦν κρίσις ἐστιν τοῦ κόσμου τούτου.

5 ἴδε ὁ ἀμνὸς τοῦ θεοῦ ὁ αἴρων τὴν ἁμαρτίαν τοῦ κόσμου.

6 For a longer discussion of this possible line of interpretation see chapter seven of my *Promise and Presence*.

7 For a previous discussion of the possible significance of this reference see my *Promise and Presence* p. 157, especially fn. 3.

8 *ST* I 13 4 & 5.

9 Anselm, *Cur Deus Homo* in *The Library of Christian Classics – A Scholastic Miscellany: Anselm to Ockham*, ed. & trans. Fairweather, E. R. (Philadelphia: Westminster Press, 1956).

10 Steve Holmes isolates a single reference in the work of Gregory the Great: 'When I look at the texts where people claim to find the fathers talking in penal substitutionary terms, I almost always find language of ransom or sacrifice. This seems to be read by some modern readers as if it should be understood as penal substitution.' Stephen R. Holmes, *Wondrous Cross: Atonement and Penal Substitution in the Bible and History* (Milton Keynes: Paternoster, 2007), p. 57.

11 For further discussion of these apparent developments see chapter eight of my *Promise and Presence* and chapter five of my *Rhythm of Doctrine*.

12 John Owen, *The Death of Death in the Death of Christ* in *The Works of John Owen*, ed. W.H. Goold, (London: Banner, 1967), vol. 10, 140–421.

13 Gustav Aulén, *Christus Victor: An Historical Study of the Three Main Types of the Idea of the Atonement*, trans. A. G. Herbert (London: SPCK, 1931)

14 '. . . the only true and steadfast Teacher, the Word of God, our Lord Jesus Christ, who did, through His transcendent love, become what we are, that He might bring us to be even what He is Himself.' Irenaeus, *Against Heresies*, V Preface in *ANF* 1, 315–567; cf. '. . . having become united with the ancient substance of Adam's formation, rendered man living and perfect, receptive of the perfect Father, in order that as in the natural [Adam] we all were dead, so in the spiritual we may all be made alive.' *Against Heresies* V 1.

15 Athanasius, *On the Incarnation*, trans. A Religious (London: Mowbray, 1953), VIII 54: Αὐτὸς γὰρ ἐνηνθρώπησεν, ἵνα ἡμεῖς θεοποιηθῶμεν.

16 For perhaps the clearest expression of this more radical interpretation of Christ's identity with us see Karl Barth's discussion of 'The Judge Judged in Our Place' in *CD* IV/1, pp. 211–283.

17 This discussion is summarised in Anthony J. Clarke's *A Cry in the Darkness*, pp. 31f.

18 See for instance W. D. Davies and Dale C. Allison, *Commentary on Matthew XIX–XXVIII*, p. 631.

19 I am grateful to Anne Clements, one of my research students, for this insight concerning the remarkable inclusivity of Matthew's Gospel.

20 This turning from God that leads inevitably to corruption and death is how Athanasius describes the human predicament: Athanasius, *On the Incarnation*, I 5.

21 Throughout this interpretation I am wholly indebted to Karl Barth and, in particular, to the passage previously mentioned: *CD* IV/1, pp. 211–283.

22 'Exchange' Copyright © 2007 E. J. Wood.

Chapter Seven: Darkness and God

1 Some manuscripts do not have *heard his cry and*.

2 Or *a son*.

3 Again there is some discussion concerning whether or not the centurion could have seen this curtain from Golgotha (not wholly depending on which curtain is intended): see Anthony J. Clarke's *A Cry in the Darkness*, pp. 30ff.

4 For a discussion of the significance of the centurion's confession see Anthony J. Clarke's *A Cry in the Darkness*, pp. 25ff.

5 For the dynamic of this Trinitarian relationship throughout the Gospel narratives see Jürgen Moltmann, *The Trinity and the Kingdom of God: The Doctrine of God*, trans. Margaret Kohl (London: SCM, 1981), pp. 61–96.

6 'In him God himself knows what it means to be forsaken by God and in trouble' Hans-Joachim Kraus, *Theology of the Psalms*, trans. Keith Crim (Minneapolis: Fortress Press, 1992), p. 189.

7 For a thorough summary of these arguments and developments see Paul L. Gavrilyuk, *The suffering of the impassible God: the dialectics of patristic thought* (Oxford: Oxford University Press, 2006).

8 So for instance, Cyril of Alexandria affirms that 'God's Word is, of course, undoubtedly impassible in his own nature and nobody is so mad as to imagine the all-transcending... nature capable of suffering . . .; *but* by very reason of the fact that he has become man, making flesh from the Holy Virgin his own, we adhere to the principles of the divine plan and maintain that he who as God transcends suffering . . ., suffered humanly in his flesh . . .' *De symbolo* 24 quoted in Paul L. Gavrilyuk, *The suffering of the impassible God*, p. 161.

9 Nestorius (d. c. 451) was deposed as Patriarch of Constantinople for preferring to speak of Mary as 'man-bearer' (ἀνθρωποτόκος) or 'Christ-bearer' (χριστοτόκος) rather than as 'God-bearer' (θεοτόκος), allegedly implying a separation of the divine from the human nature.

10 Jürgen Moltmann, *The Crucified God: The Cross of Christ as the Foundation and Criticism of Christian Theology*, trans. R.A. Wilson and J. Bowden (London: SCM, 1974).

11 For a more sustained exploration of these arguments see chapters one and two of my *Promise and Presence* or chapter one of my *Rhythm of Doctrine*.

12 For an excellent analytical discussion of some of these contributions see Anthony J. Clarke's *A Cry in the Darkness*. It is impractical to offer here an exhaustive list of contributors to this theme but a series of summary discussions can be found in N. M. de S. Cameron (ed.), *The Power and Weakness of God: Impassibility and Orthodoxy* (Edinburgh: Rutherford House, 1990).

13 '. . . there is more to this cry than an expression of Jesus' inclusive place-taking.' Peter G. Bolt, *The Cross from a Distance: Atonement in Mark's Gospel – New Studies in Biblical Theology* 18, series ed. D. A. Carson (Downers Grove: InterVarsity Press, 2004), p. 132.

14 '. . . we need to be wary lest the problem of justifying God in the face of human suffering become more important than the problem of justifying human beings in the face of human sin'. John Goldingay, 'Introduction' in *Atonement Today: A Symposium at St John's College, Nottingham*, ed. John Goldingay (London: SPCK, 1995), xi–xiii, p. xi.

15 '…whatever else the tradition is, it is not naive, and that is why the fashionable assumption that we may simply reject certain of the ancient attributes – for example impassibility – is at best patronizing to a tradition that had good reason to say the things that it did about God.' Colin E. Gunton, *Act and Being: Towards a Theology of the Divine Attributes* (London: SCM, 2002), p. 22, cf. pp.125ff.

16 Irenaeus, *Against Heresies*, in *ANF* 1, 315–567, III xvi 6.

17 In his essay, *God Crucified*, Richard Bauckham argues that since Second Temple Judaism focused on God's identity rather than the notion of divinity, on *who* rather than *what*, Christological monotheism did not constitute a break with its Jewish rootedness. Richard Bauckham, *God Crucified: Monotheism and Christology in the New Testament* (Carlisle: Paternoster, 1998).

18 נחם

19 I am grateful to Fred Cummings, one of my research students, for challenging me to take these narrative tensions with appropriate seriousness.

20 Thomas G. Weinandy, *Does God Suffer?* (Edinburgh: T&T Clark, 2000).

21 Note that, albeit differently expressed, this is also the conclusion of Paul Gavrilyuk in his *The suffering of the impassible God*.

22 *CD* II/1, pp. 257–677. Like Thomas Aquinas before him (*ST* I QQ. 3–13), Barth prefers to speak of God's 'perfections' than of God's 'attributes'.

23 Interestingly, André LaCocque links Jesus' claim to have 'made your name known' (John 17:26) to the psalmist's vow to 'declare your name' (Psalm 22:22), André LaCocque, 'My God, My God, Why Have You Forsaken Me?', p. 205.

24 For a moving account of God's identity in death and of the significance of Holy Saturday see chapter seven of Tom Smail, *Once and for All*, pp. 120–141.

Chapter Eight: Darkness and Presence

1 J. Wisdom, 'Other Minds', *Mind* (1940); reprinted in his *Other Minds* (Oxford: Blackwell, 1952); quoted in Antony Flew, *New Essays in Philosophical Theology*, ed. Antony Flew and Alasdair

MacIntyre (London: SCM, 1955), 96–99 cf. chapter ten in *Logic and Language* vol. 1, ed. Antony Flew (Oxford: Blackwell, 1951).

2 The Hebrew phrase (קול דממה דקה) is difficult to translate but 'crushing silence' is at least a possible interpretation of the text.

3 Paul Ricoeur, 'Lamentation as Prayer', p. 225.

4 I am grateful to my friend and colleague Pat Took for drawing my attention to the change in verse four of this psalm from the third person singular ('he') to the second person singular ('you').

5 'This dark night is a privation and purgation of all sensible appetites for the external things of the world, the delights of the flesh, and the gratifications of the will' *The Collected Works of Saint John of the Cross*, p. 119; 'The necessity to pass through this dark night (the mortification of the appetites and denial of pleasure in all things) to attain divine union with God arises from the fact that all of a person's attachments to creatures are pure darkness in God's sight. Clothed in these affections, people are incapable of the enlightenment and dominating fullness of God's pure and simple light; first they must reject them.' ibid., p. 123.

6 Richard J. Foster's *Freedom of Simplicity* (London: SPCK, 1981) remains a contemporary classic with respect to this aspect of Christian discipleship.

7 'Emmaus Road' Copyright © 2007 E. J. Wood.

Concluding Reflection

1 I am grateful to Andrew Percey, an undergraduate student, who was writing a dissertation on a similar theme while this book was in preparation, and who similarly focuses on the question 'where?' rather than the question 'why?': Andrew Percey, 'Just how present is God with us when we suffer: A theological reflection on the death of Hannah Choules' (Spurgeon's College, the University of Wales: Unpublished BD dissertation, 2009).

2 Significantly, Sally Nelson concludes her 2009 Whitley Lecture with a lament for Flora, her disabled daughter. Sally Nelson, *A Thousand Crucifixions*, p. 35.

Bibliography

Albright, W. F., and Mann, C. S., *The Anchor Bible – Matthew: Introduction, Translation, and Notes* (New York: Doubleday, 1971).

Anselm, *Cur Deus Homo* in *The Library of Christian Classics – A Scholastic Miscellany: Anselm to Ockham*, ed. and trans. E. R. Fairweather (Philadelphia: Westminster Press, 1956).

Athanasius, *On the Incarnation*, trans. A Religious (London: Mowbray, 1953).

Aulén, Gustav, *Christus Victor: An Historical Study of the Three Main Types of the Idea of the Atonement*, trans. A. G. Herbert (London: SPCK, 1931).

Barth, Karl, *Church Dogmatics*, vols. I–IV, Eng. trans. eds. G.W. Bromiley and T. F. Torrance (Edinburgh: T & T Clark, 1956–1975).

Bauckham, R. J., *The Theology of Jürgen Moltmann* (Edinburgh: T&T Clark, 1995).

——, *God Crucified: Monotheism and Christology in the New Testament* (Carlisle: Paternoster, 1998).

——, *Jesus and the God of Israel: 'God Crucified' and other studies on the New Testament's Christology of Divine Identity* (Milton Keynes: Paternoster, 2008).

Beasley-Murray, G. R., *John: Word Biblical Commentary 36*, gen. eds. David A Hubbard and Glenn W. Barker, NT ed. Ralph P. Martin (Waco: Word Books, 1987).

Bolt, Peter G., *The Cross from a Distance: Atonement in Mark's Gospel – New Studies in Biblical Theology 18*, series ed. D. A. Carson (Downers Grove: InterVarsity Press, 2004).

Boulton, Matthew, 'Forsaking God: A Theological Argument for Christian Lamentations.' *SJT* 55.1 (2002): 58–78.

Brown, William P., *Seeing the Psalms: A Theology of Metaphor* (Louisville: Westminster John Knox, 2002).

Brueggemann, Walter, *The Psalms and the Life of Faith*, ed. Patrick D. Miller (Minneapolis: Fortress Press, 1995).

———, *Praying the Psalms: Engaging Scripture and the Life of the Spirit* (Carlisle: Paternoster, 2007[2]).

Burrell, David B., *Deconstruction Theodicy: Why Job has nothing to say to the puzzle of suffering* (Grand Rapids: Brazos, 2008).

Burridge, Richard A., *What are the Gospels? A Comparison with Graeco-Roman Biography* (Cambridge: Cambridge University Press, 1992).

———, *Four Gospels, One Jesus? A Symbolic Reading* (London: SPCK, 1994)

Cameron, N. M. de S. (ed.), *The Power and Weakness of God: Impassibility and Orthodoxy* (Edinburgh: Rutherford House, 1990).

Carson, D. A., *From Triumphalism to Maturity: An Exposition of 2 Corinthians 10 – 13* (Grand Rapids: Baker, 1984).

Cassidy, Sheila, *Sharing the Darkness: The Spirituality of Caring* (London: DLT, 1988)

———, *Light from the Dark Valley: Reflections on Suffering and the Care of the Dying* (London: DLT 1995)

Clarke, Anthony J., *A Cry in the Darkness: The Forsakenness of Jesus in Scripture, Theology, and Experience*, Regent's Study Guides 10, gen. ed. Paul Fiddes (Oxford/Macon: Regent's Park College/Smyth & Helwys Publishing, Inc., 2002).

Colwell, John E., *Living the Christian Story: The Distinctiveness of Christian Ethics* (Edinburgh: T & T Clark, 2001).

———, *Promise and Presence: An Exploration of Sacramental Theology* (Milton Keynes: Paternoster, 2005).

———, *The Rhythm of Doctrine: a Liturgical Sketch of Christian Faith and Faithfulness* (Milton Keynes: Paternoster, 2007).

Davies, W. D., and Allison, Dale C., *A Critical and Exegetical Commentary on The Gospel According to Saint Matthew*, vol. III, *Commentary on Matthew XIX– XXVIII* (Edinburgh: T & T Clark, 1997).

Eaton, John H., *Kingship and the Psalms*, Studies in Biblical Theology, Second Series 32 (London: SCM, 1976).

Fiddes, P. S., *The Creative Suffering of God* (Oxford: Clarendon, 1988).

Flew, Antony, and MacIntyre, Alasdair, (eds.) *New Essays in Philosophical Theology*, (London: SCM, 1955).

———, (ed.) *Logic and Language* vol. 1 (Oxford: Blackwell, 1951).

Foster, Richard J., *Freedom of Simplicity* (London: SPCK, 1981).

Gavrilyuk, Paul L., *The Suffering of the Impassible God: The Dialectics of Patristic Thought* (Oxford: Oxford University Press, 2006).

Goldingay, John, (ed.), *Atonement Today: A Symposium at St John's College, Nottingham* (London: SPCK, 1995).

———, *Psalms*, vol. 1: Psalms 1 – 41, *Baker Commentary on the Old Testament Wisdom and Psalms*, ed. Tremper Longman III (Grand Rapids: Baker, 2006).

Greene-McCreight, Kathryn, *Darkness Is My Only Companion: A Christian Response to Mental Illness* (Grand Rapids: Brazos, 2006).

Gunkel, Hermann, *An Introduction to the Psalms: The Genres of the Religious Lyric of Israel*, completed by Joachim Begrich, trans. James D. Nogalski (Macon, Georgia: Mercer University Pries, 1998).

Gunton, C. E., 'The Being and Attributes of God. Eberhard Jüngel's dispute with the classical philosophical tradition.' In *The Possibilities of Theology: Studies in the Theology of Eberhard Jüngel in his Sixtieth Year*, ed. Webster, J., (Edinburgh: T & T Clark, 1994), 7–22.

———, *Act and Being: Towards a Theology of the Divine Attributes* (London: SCM, 2002).

Holmes, Stephen R., *Wondrous cross: Atonement and Penal Substitution in the Bible and history* (Milton Keynes: Paternoster, 2007).

Irenaeus, *Against Heresies* in *The Ante-Nicene Fathers*, vol. 1, ed. Alexander Roberts, James Donaldson, and A. Cleveland Coxe (Grand Rapids: Eerdmans, 1987), 315–567.

Jacquet, Louis, *Les Psaumes et le cœur de l'homme : Etude textuelle, littéraire et doctrinale, Introduction et Premier Livre du Psautier – Psaumes 1 à 41* (Belgium : Duculot, 1975)

Jeremias, Joachim, *The Eucharistic Words of Jesus*, trans. Norman Perrin (London: SCM, 1966).

John of the Cross (St), *The Collected Works of Saint John of the Cross*, trans. Kieran Kavanaugh and Otilio Rodriguez (Washington, DC: ICS Press, 1991).

Johnson, Aubrey R., *Sacral Kingship in Ancient Israel* (Cardiff: University of Wales Press, 1967²).

Jüngel, E., *God as the Mystery of the World: On the Foundation of the Theology of the Crucified One in the Dispute between Theism and Atheism*, trans. D. L. Guder (Edinburgh: T & T Clark, 1983).

Kraus, Hans Joachim, *Psalms 1–59: A Commentary*, trans. Hilton C. Oswald (Minneapolis: Augsburg Publishing House, 1988).

———, *Theology of the* Psalms, trans. Keith Crim (Minneapolis: Fortress Press, 1992).

LaCocque, André, and Ricoeur, Paul, *Thinking Biblically: Exegetical and Hermeneutical Studies*, trans. David Pellauer (Chicago and London: University of Chicago Press, 1998).

Luther, Martin, *Luther's Works* vols. 1–55, gen. ed. (vols. 1–30) Jaroslav Pelikan, gen. ed. (vols. 31–55) Helmut T. Lehmann (Philadelphia: Muhlenberg Press, 1955–75).

Mays, James Luther, *Psalms Interpretation: A Bible Commentary for Teaching and Preaching*, ed. James Luther Mays, O.T. ed. Patrick D. Miller Jr. (Louisville: Jonn Knox, 1994).

McCann, J. Clinton Jr., *A Theological Introduction to the Book of Psalms: The Psalms as Torah* (Nashville: Abingdon, 1993).

McDonald, Fergus, 'Do the Psalms speak Today?', *Scottish Bulletin of Evangelical Theology* 26.2 (2008), 170–186.

Moltmann, Jürgen, *The Crucified God: The Cross of Christ as the Foundation and Criticism of Christian Theology*, trans. R. A. Wilson and J. Bowden (London: SCM, 1974).

——, *The Trinity and the Kingdom of God: the Doctrine of God*, trans. Margaret Kohl (London: SCM, 1981).

——, *The Spirit of Life: A universal affirmation*, trans. Margaret Kohl (London: SCM, 1992).

Morris, Leon, *The Gospel According to Matthew* (Grand Rapids: Eerdmans, 1992)

Mowinckel, Sigmund, *The Psalms in Israel's Worship*, trans. D. R. Ap-Thomas, vols. I and II (Oxford: Blackwell, 1967).

Moyise, Steve, and Menken, Maarten J. J., (eds.), *The Psalms in the New Testament* (London: T & T Clark, 2004).

Nelson, Sally, *A Thousand Crucifixions: The Materialist Subversion of the Church?*, *The Whitley Lecture 2009* (Oxford: Whitley Publications, 2009).

Owen, John, *A Discourse Concerning the Holy Spirit* (1674) in *The Works of John Owen*, vol. 3, ed. W. H. Goold (London: Banner, 1965).

——, *The Death of Death in the Death of Christ* in *The Works of John Owen*, vol. 10, ed. W.H. Goold, (London: Banner, 1967), 140–421.

Sabourin, Leopold, S. J., *The Gospel According to St Matthew*, vol. 2 (Bombay: St Paul Publications, 1982).

Schaefer, Konrad, *Berit Olam: Studies in Hebrew Narrative & Poetry – Psalms*, ed. David W. Cotter, assoc. eds. Jerome T. Walsh and Chris Franke (Collegeville, MN: The Liturgical Press, 2001).

Schweizer, Eduard, *The Good News according to Mark: A Commentary on the Gospel*, trans. Donald H. Madvig (London: SPCK, 1971).

Senior, Donald P., c.p., *The Passion Narrative According to Matthew: A Redactional Study* (Leuven: Leuven University Press, 1982).

Smail, Tom, *Once and for All: A Confession of the Cross* (London: DLT, 1998).

Spurgeon, C. H., *The Soul-Winner* (London: Passmore & Alabaster, 1897).

Swinton, John, *Raging with Compassion: Pastoral Responses to the Problem of Evil* (Grand Rapids: Eerdmans, 2007).

Thomas Aquinas, *Summa Theologica*, trans. by Fathers of the English Dominican Province (Westminster, MD: Christian Classics, 1981).

Weinandy, T. G., *Does God Suffer?* (Edinburgh: T & T Clark, 2000).

Weiser, Artur, *The Psalms: A Commentary*, trans. Herbert Hartwell, The Old Testament Library, Gen. Eds. Peter Ackroyd, James Barr, John Bright, G. Ernest Wright (London: SCM, 1962).

Wisdom, J., (ed.), *Other Minds* (Oxford: Blackwell, 1952).

Yong, Amos, *Theology and Down Syndrome: Reimagining Disability in Late Modernity* (Waco: Baylor University Press, 2007).

Index of Scriptural References

Index of Names

Index of Subjects